5/10

Science
Fun at Home

Chris Maynard

A PEARSON COMPANY

LONDON, NEW YORK, MUNICH,
MELBOURNE, and DELHI

Senior Editor Sue Leonard
Project Editor Penelope York
Art Editor Jacqueline Gooden
Publishing Manager Mary Ling
Managing Art Editor Rachael Foster
Photography Steve Shott
Jacket Design Christopher Branfield
Jacket Editor Mariza O'Keeffe
DTP Designer Almudena Díaz
Picture Research Marie Osborn
Production Erica Rosen

Science Educational Consultants
Alison Porter and Frazer Swift

The scientists
Emily Couchman, Olivia Forsey, Kathryn Foster,
Aaron Gupta, Elisha Hempsted, Alexander Khan,
Hannah Leaman, Toby Leaman, Ashley Mclarty,
Peter Moggridge, Amy Wiggins

First American Edition, 2006

06 07 08 09 10 10 9 8 7 6 5 4 3 2

Published in the United States by
DK Publishing, Inc., 375 Hudson Street
New York, New York 10014

Copyright © 2001, 2006 Dorling Kindersley Limited
A catalog record for this book is available from the Library of Congress.

Previously published as
Backyard Science 0-7894-6971-5 and Kitchen Science 0-7894-6972-3

ISBN-13: 978-0-7566-1794-3
ISBN-10: 0-7566-1794-4

Color reproduction by Colourscan, Singapore
Printed and bound in China by Toppan Printing Co., Ltd

Discover more at
www.dk.com

Contents

Backyard Lab

HOW CAN AN ORDINARY BACKYARD be good for science? After all, there's not much in it. Or is there? Come to think of it, backyards are really labs of life. Even in a small plot you can spend days doing biology, zoology, meteorology, and much, much more – it's "ology" city out there! So arm yourself with the right equipment, get out, and discover your own backyard.

Whenever you pick up a bug to study it, be sure to return it to the yard unharmed.

Some scientists are very neat – others are olympic-class slobs.

When science goes well you can really get a lift out of it.

Observing a new crop on the mold farm.

You don't have to be serious to do serious science. Not a bit!

The team lines up ts tongue testers.

Coming up

In the pages ahead you will find dozens of easy lab experiments to try out in your own kitchen. Some are smelly and some may get you wet or splattered with goo – though most won't. What makes you think science isn't a messy business?

The science stuff

Now and then you'll come across a box like this. This is where you can find an explanation of the science in the experiment you just tried out.

⚠ Whenever you see this sign, it means take extra special care with the ingredients of your experiment.

⚠ This sign means that you ought to get an adult to help you do something that's a little trickier than usual.

Always check with an adult before you use any kitchen materials and equipment.

Keep a notebook handy to write down what happens when you do an experiment. You might stumble onto something that's really weird – or yucky.

*This is lab talk for vinegar, salt, and a plastic bowl.

Survival Special

WHAT DO YOU NEED TO SURVIVE? A warm home, lots of food, and a bed? Well a plant needs its comforts too. Find out what it needs and what happens if it doesn't get exactly what it wants.

Fruit cocktail

How often do you open your lunch box, eat the fruit inside it, and then throw the seeds or pits away? Next time hang on to them and try growing your own plants. Observe the whole amazing process from seed to sandwich.

Tomato seeds   Orange seeds   Apple seeds   Avocado pit

Choose your favorite fruit; tomatoes are good for this experiment since they are quick and easy to grow. Plant three pots of tomato seeds about 0.2 in (0.5 cm) below the surface of some rich compost. Water them enough so that the soil is damp – not soaking. Make some labels to stick in the pots so that you can tell them apart.

Seeds don't need light to start growing because all the food they require is stored inside them.

Put the pots into zip-top bags, which act lik mini greenhouses, and stick them in a warn dark place. After 2-3 weeks, the shoots wi appear. Take them out of their bags, give ther light, and water them regularly. You will us these three plants for your next experimen

The coco-de-mer seed

the biggest seed in th

world, is as big

as a chicken

Leave one plant in the light but deny it water.

Give one tomato plant lots of water and light.

Put a bucket over one of them but water it regularly.

Plant science

Sun CO₂

Nutrients H₂O

To survive, plants trap sunlight, breathe air (which has got carbon dioxide – CO_2 – gas in it), and drink water (H_2O). They need minerals too – just like humans need vitamins – that their roots absorb from the soil. A chemical reaction takes place in the leaves as all these ingredients are pulled together. The reaction is called photosynthesis, and this makes the food that a plant needs in order to grow.

Deny them if you dare

When your plants have grown it is time to find out what happens if they don't have water or light. You will need to deny one plant water, one light, and give the last one both, as above. Watch what happens every day. One will grow to be healthy. What happens to the other two? How quickly do they wilt, and which one wilts first? Record your results.

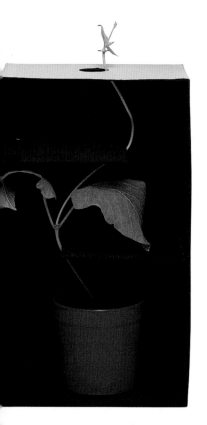

Most people think
that the tomato is a
vegetable but it is
actually a fruit

Let there be light

Plants left in the dark will starve to death. No wonder they have a knack for finding light. Place a small plant in a shoe box with a hole at the top and two pieces of cardboard on the sides to hide the light. Put on the lid and open the box once a day to see the progress. The plant will writhe until it finds the light.

Exception?

Can any plants survive without water? Not for long. Even cacti need some water. They keep going by storing it in their fleshy stems.

Captain Cook

THE YUMMIEST THING about being in command of a kitchen lab is being able to snack on the results. Perhaps it's best to wait until after your friends have eaten before you tell them they've just swallowed an emulsion of albumen!

The white stuff

The cells of egg whites stretch like microscopic balloons when you beat them. They can hold so much air that a clear yellowish puddle of egg whites will swell to a thick white foam almost four times in volume. Add sugar and, hey presto, meringue mixture.

Break four eggs in half. Slide the yolk of each egg back and forth between the two half shells while you collect the runny egg white in the bowl beneath. It's tricky, so you might need help with this step.

Use a hand whisk to beat the egg whites. As they get filled with air they completely change into a frothy, cloudlike mixture.

To make meringues you need to gently fold in about half a cup of sugar until you get a foam that's stiff but not dry. Put dollops of the mixture on a tray and ask an adult to bake them for over an hour in a very cool oven (it's more like drying than baking) heated to 270-285°F (130°-140°C).

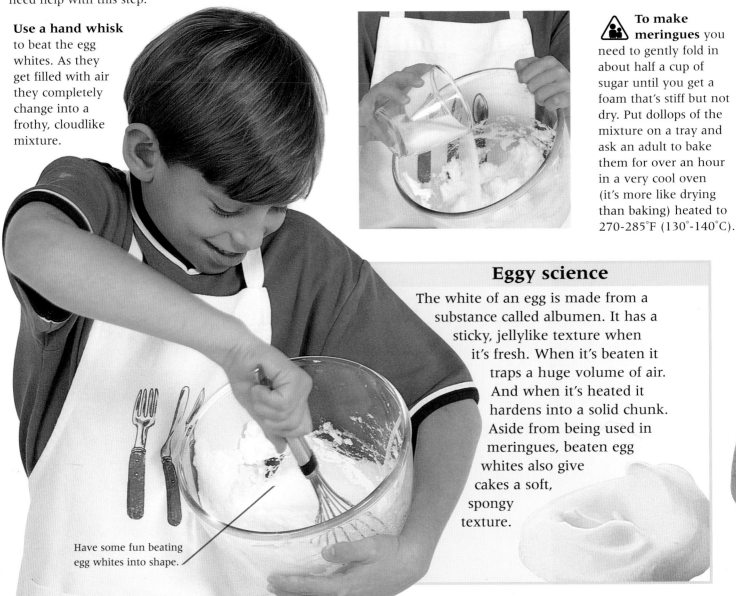

Have some fun beating egg whites into shape.

Eggy science

The white of an egg is made from a substance called albumen. It has a sticky, jellylike texture when it's fresh. When it's beaten it traps a huge volume of air. And when it's heated it hardens into a solid chunk. Aside from being used in meringues, beaten egg whites also give cakes a soft, spongy texture.

Butter fingers

In the days when people kept a cow, they often made butter by hand. Hardly anybody does it any more, yet it's not especially hard. Pour half a pint of whipping cream into a screw-top plastic container. Don't fill more than halfway. Add a pinch of salt. Put a heavy, squeaky-clean silver coin in with the cream.

Pour off the buttermilk and spoon the yellow blob onto a cloth. Wrap it up and give it a good squeeze to get rid of the last drops of liquid. You've got pure butter. And pure bliss too. So...go and make toast!

Make sure you screw the top on tight. Shake like crazy for 15 minutes or so. At first the coin rattles freely and the cream sloshes around. Then thick whipped cream forms, and the sloshing stops. The whipped cream gets thicker and stiffer. All at once it separates into a yellow blob, and a thin white liquid called buttermilk. Shake for a few seconds longer.

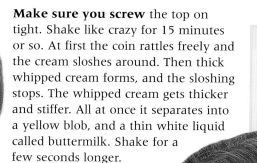

You might have aching arms from all that shaking, but you'll have fresh butter too.

Buttery science

Most people think emulsion is a kind of paint. In truth, it's any mixture where tiny droplets of one liquid hang suspended in another. Like salad dressing – oil in vinegar. Or whipped cream – butterfat in water. As you churn whipped cream, you beat droplets of butterfat until they collapse and rejoin to form a single blob of butter.

Root Power

WITHOUT ROOTS PLANTS WOULD be in lots of trouble. Plants feed themselves through roots and if they didn't have any they would fall over. Now you can prove what roots really do.

Back to the roots

Plants send their roots out under the ground to search for the water and nutrients that they need to grow. To take a look at some all-important root strands get a plant in a pot, moisten the soil, and remove it gently.

Growing up

Some stems have roots that grow above ground. They keep plants upright in the wind. They're called buttress roots and some grow as high as 30 ft (9 m).

Be very careful when you take the plant out, you don't want to break any of the hair-thin roots.

Root science

Roots have enormous strength. As they hunt for food and water they push through soil and rock like butter. Test this power yourself. Plant some seeds in an eggshell filled with damp potting soil. Put it in an eggcup and water regularly as the plants grow. In a short time the roots will feel squashed and will start to look for more room. The walls of the shell won't hold them for a moment as they search for freedom.

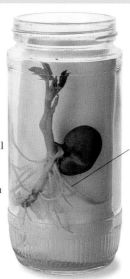

Root lab

Here's a great way to watch the progress of a root and stem – it's like having a secret window. Roll up some damp blotting paper and put it in a jar. Soak a bean overnight and place it between the paper and the glass.

The roots will start to grow first, and no matter which way up the seed is, they always grow downward.

When the roots and stem are about this big, try turning the jar upside down. What do the roots do?

Drinking science

So plants can drink, but how? As water evaporates through tiny holes (stomata, see picture below) in the leaves and petals, fresh water is drawn up from below.

In a plant there is an unbroken tower of water running from the bottom to the top, and the force that draws water up the plant from the roots to the top is known as "transpiration."

Pink drink

The best way to drink a milkshake is through a straw. Plant roots drink in pretty much the same way – though they prefer plain water. Inside the plant there are bunches of thin tubes that carry water up the roots and stems and into the leaves. Try this colorful experiment to prove it.

Does the length or the thickness of the stem make a difference?

Do some colors work better than others?

Take some white flowers and put each one in a vase. Mix different food coloring and water in the vases. Leave them for several hours to see if their stems are like straws. Some flowers work better than others, so try different ones. How long does each one take to change color? How do you think the color got to the flowers?

Pull power

How powerful is transpiration? For starters, it can lift water all the way to the top of a 164 ft (50 m) chestnut tree without batting an eyelid.

A long story

Some plants have very long root networks. The hairy roots of rye plants – a type of grass – can stretch over 370 miles (600 km) if you lay them all end to end.

Roots grow downward because they obey the law of gravity

Manic Mixtures

AN AWFUL LOT OF MIXING goes on in the kitchen, and normally you eat the results. But these strange concoctions are not for munching, they're for you to have fun with and learn from too!

Gruesome goo

This experiment works best with friends who don't mind getting gunky. Put two cups of cornstarch in a bowl and add some food coloring. While one lab partner adds about one cup of water – SLOWLY – the other mushes the mixture in the bowl by hand.

Nervous colors

Drive some innocent food coloring absolutely crazy with this experiment. Get a dish of milk, let it warm to room temperature, and then dot drops of different food coloring around it.

Dunk a toothpick into some dishwashing liquid and touch it in the center of the milk. The colors should head screaming to the sides of the dish. Dip the toothpick again but touch it to a blob of color this time and see what happens.

Use a drop of soap to ease the milk's tension

Tense science

Look at a drop of water on a scrap of foil and see how a "sausage skin" of water holds it in shape. The "skin" is called surface tension. Soap rips surface tension apart. When soap touches the milk, the surface tension at that point snaps, but it is as strong as ever in the rest of the bowl. That's why the milk (and the colors) rush toward the side of the dish.

Get ahold of some kitchen utensils and see how the goo works when you push it through holes or try to spoon it around.

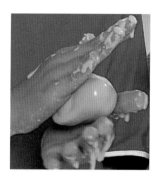

Pick up a blob and roll it in your hands to make a solid ball. Stop and let the ball rest. It should slip through your fingers.

Gooey science

Your goo is sometimes a solid and sometimes a liquid. That's because cornstarch doesn't really dissolve. It only forms tiny solid pieces that hang suspended in the water. Scientists call this strange type of liquid a colloid. Colloids do weird things. The harder you press, the firmer they feel. But when you ease off and open your hand, they run and drip. The secret of handling colloids is this: slow for flow, hard for solid.

Silly business

In the middle of World War II, an American engineer began to look for a cheap alternative to rubber. He made a goo that stretched and bounced better than rubber, but was much too soft and squishy to make into tires. One day a toy store owner saw someone playing with the goo. It looked like fun stuff, so he bought some, rolled it into balls, and sold them packed in plastic eggs. He called it Silly Putty®. Kids snapped up 750,000 sets in three days and started a toy sensation that's still in the stores today.

Squeeze a handful hard, then stop squeezing and open your hand.

Plunge your hands in and mess with your goo.

Floating Around

PEOPLE HAVE BEEN STEALING GOOD IDEAS from nature since the Stone Age. That's why parachutes and helicopters look suspiciously like some of the seeds that float across the backyard now and again.

Parachute copycat
A parachute works in the same way as the dandelion seed. The canopy opens, which makes the fall to the ground slower so that skydivers land softly – most of the time.

Get away seed

Why do seeds abandon their parents? Because big plants hog space, light, and water. Seeds must get as far away as possible to survive. Dandelion and thistle seeds have fluffy parachutes that trap the wind and waft them all over the place.

The seed is the weight at the bottom of the dandelion parachute.

The piece of modeling clay, like the seed, weighs the parachute down slightly to keep the canopy open.

Make your own parachute

by cutting out a square piece of material. Tie a piece of string to each corner and attach the ends together around a piece of modeling clay, as shown. Let it fall from a height. The canopy opens, traps the air, and it falls slowly. If it is windy, how far does it travel before it hits the ground?

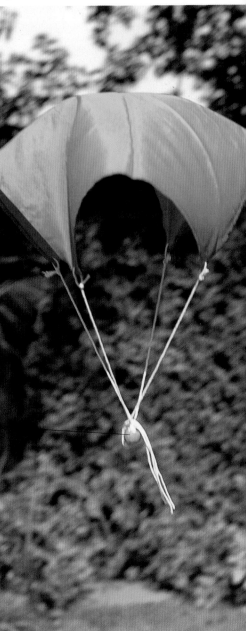

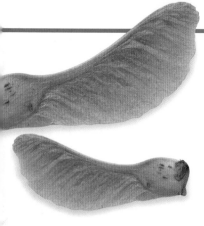

Copter copycat

Have you ever noticed maple seeds spinning around and around as they fall to the ground? They work like a helicopter – they have spinning wings that use air to fly. Try making your own helicopter wings.

In a spin

Make your own minicopter and see how far you can get it to spin away from you.

Copy this minicopter pattern onto a sheet of stiff paper – about as tall as a piece of 8^1/$_2$ x 11 inch paper.

Cut along the solid lines and fold along the dotted lines. Fold the top flaps over in opposite directions.

Fold the bottom flap up and pin it with a paper clip. The added weight helps the minicopter to spin.

Watch as your minicopter floats through the air. The falling blades hit the air, forcing it outward with a sideways push. As the air flow shifts, the copter starts to spin. A maple seed shifts air in the same way except that the tip of the seed is bent slightly inward, which forces it to spin.

The balsam flower just needs an animal to brush against it, or a gust of wind to encourage it to send its seeds flying.

Dispersal science

Long before humans, flowering plants were busy figuring out ways to spread their seeds far and wide. They came up with three ways: animals, water, and the wind.

Birds and beasts

Animals and birds do an effective job of dispersal by having seeds cling to their fur or ride in their gut after they swallow them. Burrs hook themselves on to fur like velcro – in fact the idea for velcro came from burrs.

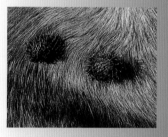

Seed passengers

Lotus plants grow in water and rely on the river to carry away their seeds. Poppies have pods like tiny pepperpots. They're full of seeds that are flung out when the wind rocks the plant. The balsam flower holds its seeds in little catapults. When jiggled, the seeds explode away.

Lotus plant

Opium poppy

Balsam flower

Double Bubble Trouble

YOU MAY NOT REALIZE how much science there is in blowing a soap bubble. That's probably because your bubbles have been too small for any really good experiments. If so, just wait until you get your hands on these giants.

Monster bubbles

Lots of people use little jars of bubble mixture to blow golf ball-size bubbles. But now it's time to think bigger. A LOT BIGGER. It's time to make some mega-bubbles longer than your arm and bigger than your head.

Mix half a cup of dishwashing liquid with a couple of pitchers of water in a large dish. The mixture will be better if you make it a day before you use it. Pull a metal coat hanger into a roundish shape. Plunge it into the mixture and pull it out slowly. Once you're sure you've been successful, wobble the bubble around to make fun shapes.

Bubble science

When you blow air into a soapy film it swells like a balloon. Finally it snaps shut and traps a puff of air inside itself to form a bubble. From being horribly stretched, the bubble now tries to relax to its original size. The air inside makes this impossible. So it forms the least stretchy shape it can – a ball. That's why all bubbles, no matter what they look like at first, end up sphere shaped rather than as boxes, cones, or doughnuts.

Color dome

Bubbles play wonderful tricks with light – just like rainbows. Here's an experiment to prove it.

Tape a flashlight to the bottom of a clear plastic lid. Hold it upright and spoon a little bubble mix onto the lid.

The flashlight shines up through the bubbles to create a rainbow-colored dome.

A soap bubble is less than 1 millionth of an inch thick as it starts to pop

Stick a straw into the bubble mix and gently blow some bubbles to make a bubble dome. Step into a dark room and switch the flashlight on. Take a good look at the bubbles. What colors do you see swirling about? Do they ever change? What colors do you see just before a bubble pops?

Try dunking funnels or other kitchen utensils into the bubble mixture and blow air through them.

Color science

All bubbles are a sandwich of soap and water. As they reflect light from a flashlight you can see the colors of the rainbow swirling on their walls. If you blow gently on a bubble, the colours change as the walls get thinner. When the bubble walls are at their thinnest the colors disappear, so just before a bubble pops, it appears to go black.

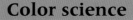

Birdwatch

BIRDS ARE HAPPY WHEN THE BACKYARD is full of tender worms and beetles. And if humans leave feeders for them – even better. Get them into your backyard with food they can't resist then study their behavior.

Bird chef

Bird food is nothing like the food we like to eat – but birds find it beak-smackingly good. It's packed with goodies to keep birds stocked up with the vitamins and fats that they need.

Take various kitchen scraps – oats, cooked rice, leftover vegetables, nuts, birdseed, bacon rind, or breadcrumbs – and mix them into a bowl. Ask an adult to pour some hot shortening into the bowl and mix until it is a gooey mess.

Fill a small flowerpot with the gooey mixture, stick a small twig through the middle of it, and put it in the fridge to set. When it is hard, ease out the set mixture. Tie some string around the stick and hang it on a branch.

You will need a large needle to thread the string through. But be careful not to prick yourself.

Note the different colors of the birds and identify them later.

Getting spotty

Three things will make you better at spotting birds – a pair of binoculars, a notebook, and lots of patience. How many different birds can you spot in a day, or in a week? Keep a log.

Take a handful of nuts and carefully thread them onto a piece of string. Peanuts work very well. The birds can easily crack open the nut necklace.

Bird food favorites

In winter birds can starve because it is so difficult to find food. There are very few bugs and seeds around. So you might be a lifesaver if you hang food out. Fatty foods, such as bacon rind and shortening, are particularly good for building body fat. Birds will appreciate food in warm weather too. So continue to hang food out and enjoy watching bird behavior all year.

Did you know?

Swifts spend almost their entire life flying. They only land to lay eggs and to look after their young.

Bird care

In addition to hanging feeders, fill a bowl of fresh water and put it nearby. The birds will enjoy splashing in it as they wash, as well as drinking it.

Warning! Don't put salty foods out for the birds. Their bodies can't take it.

Push the bird mixture tightly into a large pinecone and hang it up.

Try a mix of different nuts threaded onto a piece of string.

When you tie the food to the tree, make sure you tie the knots tightly – birds can be heavy.

A milk carton makes a fantastic birdseed holder for small birds. Simply cut a hole in one side, fill it with birdseed or nuts, and attach some string.

21

Tower of Strength

THE SCIENCE OF BUILDING is incredibly clever. Simply by changing the shape of your materials you can make them stronger, and by gluing small bricks together you can make one stable, solid object.

First build a tower out of plain sugar cubes. Stack one on top of the other and see how high you can pile them before they fall over.

Sticky bricks

The secret of building structures that don't fall down is to use bricks AND cement. Try the recipe below to cement sugar cubes together in sixes. Then cement the sixes in layers. How high can this tower rise before it starts to wobble?

Tired of towers? Why not make an igloo with your leftover sugar bricks.

⚠ The cement smells good enough to eat – but don't! Raw eggs have to be cooked before they can be eaten.

To make grade A sugar cement mix three egg whites with about one cup of icing sugar in a bowl, beat it into a thick paste, and slather it on. The thicker the cement the stronger the tower will be. Keep the mixture in an airtight jar so that it doesn't dry out.

Building bridges

It's obvious that a sheet of paper can't hold up a heavy load. Or can it? If you were an engineer you'd know a good few tricks for building strong paper bridges.

Tape a piece of construction paper over the top of two tin cans to build a bridge. How many carrot slices can the construction paper bridge hold before it collapses?

Suspension bridges

These bridges use cables strung across tall towers to hold up heavy loads. The shape is so strong that it's the best way to span long distances. This picture shows the famous Golden Gate Bridge in San Francisco, which is the fifth longest bridge in the world. The longest is the Akashi Kaikyo Bridge in Japan, which spans nearly 7,000 ft (about 2,000 m).

Keep piling on the carrots to see what shape makes the strongest bridge.

Try the different bridge shapes below and see which is the strongest. The corrugated bridge holds up a load well, because by pleating the paper you turn it into a set of upright lengths. Each upright has a lot more strength than a flat sheet. Together they make your bridge strong enough to take a huge load of carrot slices.

Arch bridges

Arch bridges are one of the oldest types of bridges. They have an arc-shaped span in the middle. The arc carries weight along it's curve and out toward the two ends. This makes them stronger than a beam bridge because the two ends carry most of the load. Like this there's not much chance of the middle sagging.

Bridge science

A beam bridge is held up by pillars. The corrugated sheet makes a beam bridge, so does a girder. But an even stronger shape for bridges is an arch.

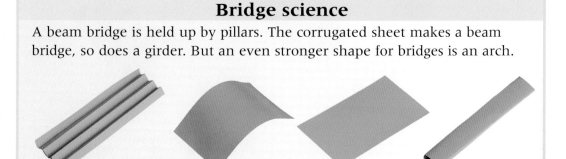

Corrugated beam   Arch   Flat beam   Girder beam

Feathered Friends

WHAT DOES A BACKYARD HOPPING with birds make you think of? Feathers? Eggs? Now imagine wha a scientist thinks. Why do birds fly rather than nosedive downward? What is inside an egg?

What keeps them up?

Without feathers, a bird would be cold, wet, unable to fly, and extremely thin. Birds have down feathers, body feathers, tail, and wing feathers. What is each one for, and how do they work?

How do flight feathers work?

Pin the shaft of a wing feather loosely to a stick, keeping the narrow edge facing you. Blow over the narrow edge of the feather and watch how it lifts. Now turn the feather around. What does it do this time?

Flying science

If the feather is from a wingtip it has a curved surface. As a bird flies, air over the curved upper part flows faster than air that is passing below it. The difference in air speed above and below lifts up the whole feather. This lift keeps birds from crash landing.

Flight feathers are smooth and glossy. They are made from lightweigh strands hooked tightly together.

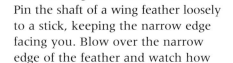

Body feathers are sometimes patterned at the top. This can be for camouflage or simply to show off.

Body feathers are downy and warm like a comforter. But they don't have much to do with flying. Some body feathers trap air to help insulation.

Tail feather help birds to steer and balance as they fly.

Flight patterns

Birds fly in a lot of different ways. Study their flight patterns next time you are birdwatching and draw how they fly. A swift flys in all directions and swoops and soars. A finch flaps then glides for a while.

Swift flight

Finch flight

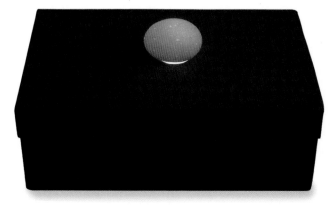

Egg science

It's unlikely that you'll see any fertilized eggs unless you go to a farm. Farmers use a metal can, very similar to your box, called a "candler" to tell if an egg is fertilized. If the yolk looks more solid then there is a chance a chick will grow.

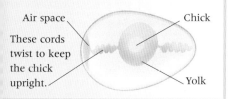

Air space

These cords twist to keep the chick upright.

Chick

Yolk

Eggs-ray eyes

How do you look inside a chicken egg without breaking it? Paint a shoe box black. Cut out a small hole in the lid. Place a flashlight in the box shining up through the hole. Go somewhere dark, turn on the flashlight, and put an egg over the hole. What do you see?

The smallest egg of all is the bee hummingbird's. End to end it can be just 0.4 in long (1 cm) – about fingernail size.

The biggest egg in the world is an ostrich egg. You'd need to crack open at least a dozen chicken eggs to fill it up

Try making your own nest and imagine only using a beak and two feet.

Lichen and moss for camouflage.

Down feathers for insulation.

⚠ Nesting place

Never go near a bird's nest while it is full of eggs. If you touch the nest the mother bird will abandon it. Always watch from a distance. Take a look at the nest above. A bird uses many materials to make a safe, insulated home for its brood.

Hatching out

A mother bird sits on her eggs keeping them warm until they hatch. If you are lucky enough to see a nest in a tree, watch it from a distance. When the time comes for the chicks to hatch they have to work pretty hard to get out.

As the air in the end of the egg gets used up the chick pokes holes in the blunt end using the sharp tip of its beak.

It shoves hard with its feet to flip off the cap of the shell. When it breaks the chick starts to wriggle out.

Within a few hours it runs around feeding itself. It does what takes us five years in a matter of a few hours.

Moldy Stuff

IF YOU ALREADY HAVE WARM feelings for mushrooms and fungi, then you'll really love mold. They all belong to the same family of plants but not one of them has any seeds. Instead, these plants grow from spores.

Spore print

Mold, like mushrooms, grows from dust-sized specks. Take a spore print from a mushroom to get a good look at some spores, and to make an amazing pattern.

⚠️ **Get ahold of the biggest** mushroom you can buy. Never use wild mushrooms, because they can be poisonous. Cut off the stalk. Set the mushroom face down on a piece of cardboard, cover with a bowl, and leave it for a few days. The spores can range from white to black, so use a piece of cardboard with a contrasting color so that the spores show up well.

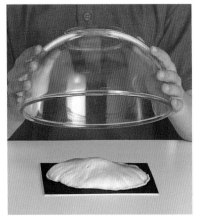

You'll be left with a pale, powdery ring when you take the bowl away and lift the mushroom up. These are the spores. Normally they blow away in the wind, settle somewhere damp, and start to grow into new mushrooms.

A fine sprinkling of mushroom spores.

Moldy science

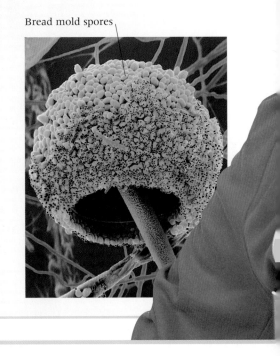

Bread mold spores

Mold is a plant – a cousin of fungus. But instead of nice rich soil, mold prefers damp, rotting things to feast on. Mold grows as a tangle of threads. Inside are colonies of spore cases. Each case is a tiny pinhead with thousands of spores inside it. After the case breaks open, the spores sail away on the air looking for more moist food to land on and grow.

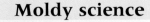

Moldy bread

Get moldy!

Want to set up a mold ranch experiment? You'll need chunks of leftover food like bread, cheese, vegetables, and fruit. Don't use meat or fish as they get highly stinky.

Dip the chunks in water. (Mold hates being dry.) Put them in a glass jar with a screw top and shut it tight. Tape the lid closed so nothing gets in or out. Put the jar away where nobody will find its disgusting innards and throw them away.

Yummy mold

Mold belongs to the fungus family – just like mushrooms and mildew. It commonly grows on food, or the rotting remains of animals and plants. Most often we throw out food if it gets moldy. But when certain cheeses, like the ones with blue or green veins in them, get moldy they take on a delicious flavor. That's when we eat mold.

Thanks to a mold we get the lifesaving drug called penicillin

Soon a fuzzy garden will start to grow. It's your mold crop.

⚠ Special cheeses are fine to eat but mold isn't. Make sure you tape up the jars at the start of this experiment, and do not open them before you throw them away.

After a few days you'll start to see patches of white, green, or blue growing on the food. They are mold. Which kinds of food got moldy first? Was the mold smooth or fuzzy? Did everything in the jar go moldy? Throw away the jar and the moldy remains when you're finished with them.

Sound Effects

Ask an adult to tie the string securely to the shaft of wood.

STAND PERFECTLY STILL and listen hard. What can you hear? From the loudest clap of thunder to the scuttling of a mouse, our ears can identify sounds all around us like radar collecting information. But what makes the sound, and how do we come to hear them?

Make sure no one is standing near you when you swing.

Bull roarer

Here's a way to make the air vibrate so that it roars. Take a ruler-sized slat of wood and ask an adult to make a hole in one end. Tie a piece of string through the hole and swing it around your head at top speed. Can you feel the air vibrate as the wood roars?

Wave watch

Sound waves work like water wav[es] – they'd look like them too if they were visible. Drop some water into a bowl and watch the waves sprea[d] out. Sound spreads just like this.

Sound science

Sound is a set of vibrations. They travel through the air in waves, just like water waves in a bowl. Your ears pick up these vibrations at your ear drum. The bull roarer vibrates the air as it spins and produces sound waves that "roar." You can also feel sound vibrations by touching your throat when you talk.

Sound game

Can you tell where a sound comes from? Not sure? Try this game. Blindfold one person and then place two or more friends around her. Take turns clapping, and the blindfolded person must point to where he thinks the sound comes from. It's not as easy as it sounds!

Take a big breath and blow the whistle for as long as you can.

Some jets can go faster than the speed of sound

High-low

A train hurtles into a station with a high-pitched roar that gets deeper the moment it thunders past you. Why? The answer is the Doppler effect. Ask a friend to ride past fast, blowing a whistle. Fast-moving objects squeeze sound waves traveling in front of it, so they sound higher. Then they stretch them out behind, making them deeper.

Thunder clap

Sound is no slouch. But it is slow compared to the speed of light. That is why in a thunderstorm the lightning appears first, even though thunder booms and sends out its sound waves at exactly the same time. Sound travels 0.5 miles (0.3 km) in one second. During the next storm, count, in seconds, from when you see the lightning until you hear the thunder. You can then work out how far away the storm is.

Echo-o-o-o

An echo is a sound that has bumped headfirst into something and then bounced back. Bats use echoes to find their prey. As they fly in the dark they let out high-pitched squeaks that bounce off objects in front of them. Their ears pick up the faint echoes so they can work out where insects are flying in the dark.

Sour Power

LEMONS ARE PACKED with sour-tasting juice. It is also a natural acid. This makes lemons the perfect things for all sorts of fruity scientific experiments.

Lemon fizz

Most batteries are heavy tubes packed with chemicals. But other things can make electricity flow, too, and they don't look a bit like batteries. Take lemons, for example.

Shocking science

What happened is that you created a natural battery. The science is the same as for man-made batteries. Lemon juice is a weak acid (that's why it has a sour taste). It reacts with the two different metals you stick into it to make an electric current. As long as a lemon has juice it has power.

Get a fresh lemon. Stick a short piece of copper wire into one side. Unbend a steel paper clip and plunge it into the lemon next to the copper wire. Now gently touch the free ends of the wire and paper clip to your tongue. The tingle you feel is a current of pure electricity. Never use batteries or different wires for this experiment, as they could be dangerous.

Lemon preserve

Mighty lemons can do a lot more than make electricity. They can also stop apples from turning brown. To start with, ask someone to cut an apple into quarters for you.

A lemon is a type of berry

Squeeze lemon juice onto two quarters. Leave one quarter with lemon juice and one without on the table. Put the other quarters in the fridge. Look at them a few hours later – the untreated slices will have gone brown.

No juice/ no fridge

Juice/ no fridge

No Juice/ in fridge

Juice/ in fridge

Lemon float

Here's a way to show that lemons float – except when you peel them. Put a lemon in water, and watch it bob happily on the surface. Right now it is lighter than water.

Now pare the rind with a peeler. Back into the water it goes...and sinks. When you took off the rind you removed the lemon's life jacket, for the rind is full of thousands of tiny air bubbles. Take them away, and the flesh that's left is heavier than water.

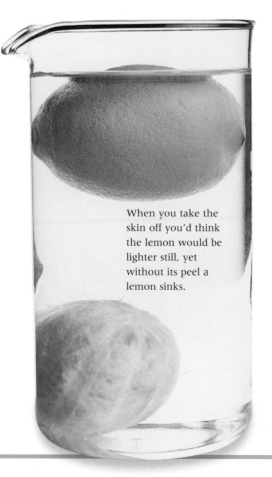

When you take the skin off you'd think the lemon would be lighter still, yet without its peel a lemon sinks.

Discolored science

When an apple is sliced the "cells" within it get ripped open. This means that the chemicals inside the cells can react with oxygen in the air, which turns the apple flesh brown. The acid in lemon juice (it's called citric acid) stops these chemicals in their tracks. Chilling the chemicals stops them too, which is why the apple quarters in the fridge don't get nearly so brown.

Smells fishy

How do you keep a fish from smelling? Cut off its nose! How do you keep your hands from smelling after you handle fresh fish? Use lemon juice! Fishy scent comes from chemicals in the body oils of fish. It's hard to get rid of it with soap and water. But if you rub your hands with lemon juice, the acid changes the fish oil chemicals so that they rinse off under running water.

Bug Safari

THE FIRST THING PEOPLE NOTICE about bugs is this – boy there are a lot of them. We suspect there are zillions, although nobody can count that high. And what's their secret? It's that they can eat anything and live anywhere. Check it out in your backyard.

Glass cage

Try studying bugs up close, and you'll find they won't stay still. Look carefully under logs and stones, place the bugs gently in a jar, and put muslin over the top. (Set them free afterward.)

Night shift

Bugs that scuttle about by day aren't hard to find. But you need cunning to follow the night crawlers. Cut a grapefruit in half and scoop out the fleshy parts. Put the halves, face down, in your backyard overnight. Check in the morning to see which bugs dropped by for a snack.

A feasting woodlouse

Safe haven

If you want to look at a live bug, make a special observatory. Dig a hole, drop a yogurt cup inside it, and put in a piece of food – a chunk of cheese or some cookie crumbs. Balance a sheet of wood on four pebbles over the observatory to keep the bugs safe and dry.

Study your bugs carefully, then free them.

Swap your food now and then. Which kind attracts the most bugs?

Pooter power

Think of a vacuum cleaner without an engine. That's a pooter. It's a handy, harmless way to gently lift up small insects by using the power of human breath – but don't worry, you won't suck any into your mouth by mistake!

Cut two lengths of tubing – one 20 in (50 cm), and one half the size. Tie a piece of muslin around one end of the short tube with a rubber band.

Using tape, attach a piece of cardboard to the top of a jar, with two holes in the top for the tubes. Use modeling clay to wedge the tubes tight.

Bug science

Scientists have named about a million insect species, and some people believe that there may be millions more to be identified. Not all bugs are insects, however – only those with six legs and bodies divided into three parts – like this beetle.

Centipedes and millipedes are not insects because they have many legs. You can find them living under stones and logs.

Hold the long tube above the bug, give a short suck, and vacuum it into the pooter.

The muslin stops you from swallowing the bug.

Fizzical Reactions

THIS IS THE SORT OF THING RESEARCH chemists like to do – mix two different chemicals to cook up a third. In this case the chemist is you, and the new chemical you're going to make is a very common gas.

Get some vinegar and add a little red food coloring to it. Use a funnel to half fill a small plastic bottle with baking soda. Now you are ready to create your own volcano.

Chemical eruptions

When we say "volcano" most people think of burning lava. But have you ever heard of a cold volcano? Well you have now, because with this experiment you end up making fizz not fire.

Put the bottle with the baking soda in it in the middle of a large dish or tray. Pile sand around it to make a mini-mountain.

⚠ **Pour the red** vinegar mixture into the top of the volcano and prepare for a fizzing chemical reaction. If you get any of the "lava" on your skin, wash it off right away.

Inflated ideas

How can you use a liquid to inflate a balloon? Try this chemical concoction. It will leave you amazed, but not breathless. Stand back and watch the balloon blow up as if by magic.

Half fill a big bottle with a mixture that is half vinegar and half water.

Keep the top of the balloon dangling low until you are ready to inflate it. Then lift the balloon up so that the powder falls into the bottle. Now count the bubbles, thousands and thousands of them. And look what happens to the balloon.

Use a funnel to fill a balloon with baking soda. Then stretch the end of the balloon tightly over the top of the bottle.

Gassy science

Why did the volcano erupt and the balloon expand? Because the soda (sodium bicarbonate) and vinegar (acetic acid) reacted and made a gas called carbon dioxide. A zillion bubbles of it were released, making both the lava flow and the balloon swell up.

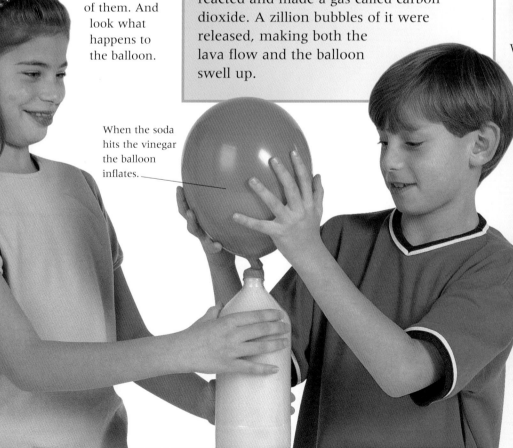

When the soda hits the vinegar the balloon inflates.

Gas guzzlers

The gas you made in these experiments is the same carbon dioxide that soft drink manufacturers put in their cans and bottles. In the factory, they bottle soft drinks at high pressure. The gas is squashed so hard that it all dissolves in the liquid.

When you open the top of a bottle, the pressure drops. There's a whoosh of gas and a cloud of bubbles starts to escape from within. They make your soft drink carbonated and taste good. They're also why you burp so loudly after guzzling a can of it. The scientist who invented soft drinks lived in Britain in the 1700s. His name was Joseph Priestly. He found that bubbling carbon dioxide through water gave it a bright and sparkling taste.

⚠Backyard Guests

IF YOU WANT TO GET TO KNOW the creatures that live in your backyard, why not make them feel so welcome they'll want to stay. By watching them going about their daily business, you can get a real feeling for how they live.

Caterpillar ranch

Observing butterflies is tricky, but caterpillars are much easier to keep an eye on. The best time to find caterpillars is in spring or early summer. Check out what species the caterpillar is and what it eats, then make a home for it in an empty tub with lots of the food it likes. The really fun part is watching them turn into butterflies and heading off into the wild.

Line the tub with paper towels and spray them lightly with water. Leave the caterpillars on the leaves or twigs that they live on and transfer everything into your tub. Feed them fresh leaves every day, keep the tub moist, and place muslin over the top

Green is not a usual flower color. How many bees try it?

Caterpillar science

A butterfly lays caterpillar eggs on leaves that will come in handy later. When the caterpillar emerges it eats the leaves it is born on.

Honey, I trained the bees!

All summer long, bees drone from flower to flower gathering nectar. Use some fake nectar and encourage honeybees to visit your backyard. Cut three colored flower shapes out of cardboard. Place a bottle lid in the center of each one. Fill the blue flower lid with sugary water and the others with plain water. Leave them outside. When a bee has found some nectar, it flies back to its nest and does a waggle dance to tell the others where to get it. Do they go for the right flower?

Are bees smart – do they go for the right one?

When the caterpillar is fully grown it turns into a pupa, which looks a bit like a dry piece of wood hanging off a leaf.

How many bees are fooled by the plain water?

Snail expedition

Snails don't rush. But they are determined creatures, and they get where they want to in the end, leaving a slimy trail behind them. Collect some snails and paint a number on their shells. Put them back where you found them and keep track of their movements through the day. Which is the champion traveler? Where do they rest in your backyard?

Inside the pupa a change takes place. The tissue of the caterpillar's body is broken down, and new organs and tissues develop. After a few weeks the butterfly is ready to struggle out. It looks bedraggled at first but after a few hours the wings dry and harden so that it can fly.

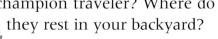

Be careful not to get any paint on the snail itself, and wash your hands after handling them.

Acid Tests

SUCK ON A LEMON, or drip a drop of vinegar on your tongue. Why do they have that mouth-puckering taste? It's because both are weak acids, and all acids taste sour. Bases are the opposite of acids. Weak ones taste bitter and feel slightly soapy. Lots of detergents are made with bases.

Get a jar of pickled cabbage and drain the red juice into a bowl.

Crazy cauldron

This experiment mixes an acid and a base and gets some really fizzing and smelly results.

Acid rain

When traffic and chimney fumes mix with rain, they may make it as acidic as lemon juice. The trouble with acid rain is that it reacts with much of what it touches, including buildings and trees.

⚠ **Add baking soda** to the bowl. The liquid will fizz and gradually change color. Then add some vinegar to the bowl. The liquid will fizz and change color again. In this experiment the cabbage juice fizzes when you add the baking soda (a base) because pickled cabbage juice has vinegar in it – which is an acid.

Pink and blue

The easy way to tell acids and bases apart is with an indicator. It's a smart substance that can't be fooled. Plain red cabbage juice is an excellent indicator, but you'll have to get an adult to help you make it. It always changes to pink when it comes into contact with an acid and blue when it meets a base.

⚠️ **Ask a grown-up** to chop up a head of red cabbage and put it to soak in a pot of hot water. After a few hours, drain off the reddish purple soup. Set up four jars of cabbage juice and rummage through the kitchen looking for acidic things to turn it pink and basic things to make it go blue.

Lemon juice is a weak acid, and so it turns the indicator red.

Distilled water isn't acid or a base. It's neutral, so the indicator doesn't change color.

Baking soda forms a weak base, so the indicator goes blue.

Milk of magnesia is a strong base, so the indicator goes green.

Coming clean

Many kitchen materials are made from bases. This experiment uses baking soda, which works as a mild cleaner, and aluminum foil to bring a shine to silverware.

⚠️ **Put a cupful of baking soda** in a bowl with six cups of boiling water. Get an adult to pour the boiling water in for you. Stir the mixture until the soda dissolves and add some strips of aluminum foil.

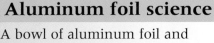

Aluminum foil science

A bowl of aluminum foil and baking soda mixture creates an electric current – just like a car battery. It lifts the tarnish off the silver and deposits it onto the foil. As a result the silver comes out sparkling.

Put some silverware in the mixture and in no time at all it should be sparkly clean. Rinse the silverware and give it a good polish. Then bask in the gratitude of your parents for polishing the silver (make sure you have their permission first).

Use science to help you do kitchen chores

Night Life

BUGS HAVE ALL THE LUCK. Just as humans are getting tucked in bed, millions of insects are putting on their party clothes to go out for the night. Of course, it's just common sense. There are a lot fewer birds and people around to annoy them.

Bats sleep during the day by hanging upside down.

Moths love to sip sugary liquids with their long tongues.

Moth ball

Moths will think that you're holding a grand ball if you serve them this delicious cocktail one night. Paint some juice concentrate on a tree, shine a flashlight on it when it gets dark, and wait for your guests to show up. How many moths come to your feast

Night noises

Except for snoring, night ought to be a time of peace and quiet. If only! Go into the backyard at dusk and keep very still. Depending on where you live, you may hear frogs croak, owls hoot, mosquitoes whine, crickets rub their knees, and, if you are lucky, the strangled bark of a fox. Keep a logbook of any nocturnal sounds that you can identify.

The hoot of an owl is a common sound at night.

Owls can turn their heads 270° each way!

Small, round paw prints such as these may be cats. A silver glistening trail is a snail or a slug.

Night creatures

Unlike us humans, many animals sleep during the day and are active when it gets dark. Long ago, small mammals moved around in darkness to avoid being caught by hungry dinosaurs, and some have remained nocturnal to this day. This means that hunters such as foxes and owls have become active at night in order to catch them.

Glow by night

There are thousands of living things that glow at night like lightbulbs. The most common is the firefly, which is actually a beetle. It has a chemical in its body that makes it glow. Each species has its own code of signals, based on flashes, by which fireflies can "talk" to each other. Some scientists have measured the timing between flashes and so have learned to imitate the signals.

Animal trackers

Wild animals are often shy so only appear at night. They skidaddle the moment they hear you coming. Here's a way to ensure that they leave their calling card. Lay a pile of sand on the ground, dampen it a little, and make sure it is smooth. You could put a bit of bait on it. Next morning check for any tracks.

Dew science

On clear, still nights when the air gets chilly, water vapor in the air becomes dew, which forms near the ground. Early in the morning, go outside and check out the dewy spider's webs with each strand glistening with moisture.

Smooth as silk

Amazingly enough, soft silk is produced from the hard cocoon of the silk moth. Each cocoon unravels into a thread of silk that can be over 0.6 miles (1 km) long in total.

Sinking Feeling

DO YOU THINK EVERYONE in your class is dense? Well they are, because everything has density, it's just that some things are more dense or less dense than others – just as these experiments show.

On the level

Corn syrup, water, and oil all have different densities, and because less dense liquids always float on more dense ones you can make your own density cocktail (not for drinking).

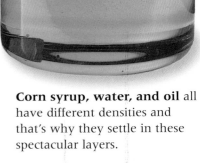

Use food coloring to color the water.

Pour some corn syrup into a pitcher until it is about a quarter full. Then add the same amount of vegetable oil and the same amount of colored water.

Dense science

If you weigh a piece of metal and a piece of cork that are the same size you will find that the metal weighs more. That means that the metal is more dense than the cork. That's why it sinks deeper in the pitcher than either the cork or the grape.

Corn syrup, water, and oil all have different densities and that's why they settle in these spectacular layers.

Is a cork more dense than oil? Where does the grape settle? Does the nut sink or swim?

The liquids separate into three layers, with the densest at the bottom and the least dense on top. Collect three objects – a metal nut, a cork, and a grape – drop them in and test which is most and least dense.

Oily diving

A drop of oil is less dense than a drop of water. That's why it floats on top. Because oil and water don't mix well, here's a great diving trick you can play with them.

Take a large jar, and pour in some water about four fingers deep. Then add a finger or two of oil. When everything settles, which is the top layer?

Add a drop or two of food coloring. Does the color end up in the oil or in the water?

The oil hitches a ride with the salt and sinks down into the water.

Sprinkle some salt on the surface. What happens next? You can make the oily diving last as long as you want just by adding more salt each time.

Salty science

Salt is heavier than oil or water. It sinks as you sprinkle it on, and it carries a blob of oil down with it. The salt dissolves when it reaches the water. The oil is set free and at once floats back up to the top.

Straw float

Pack a lump of modeling clay on the end of a drinking straw and you get a hydrometer (a tool that measures density). Put it in different liquids: water, oil, liquid soap, and see how well it floats. If the liquid is dense, it floats high. If not dense, it floats low. Which of your test liquids is the densest?

Lava lamps

This weird invention was dreamed up by a man who knew that wax became less dense when heated. He took a tall jar, put some colored wax at the bottom, filled it with liquid and set it on top of a light bulb. The hot bulb melted the wax, and blobs of it rose up the jar. At the top they cooled, became denser and sank – only to be warmed on the bottom and rise again.

Big Splash!

YOU CAN TAKE A BATH IN IT. You can brush your teeth in it. You can drink it. Even better, you can also use water to show off how much you know about science. Find out how amazing water can be and prepare to get wet!

Water whirl

If you hold a cup of water upside down it empties out, right? Not always. Fill a bucket of water about a quarter full and with a swift action swing it up and over your head in a full circle, over and over again. What happens to the water?

Don't be timid with the bucket, give it a really good swing.

Centrifugal science

The water stays in the bucket because it's held in by centrifugal force. When the bucket swings in a circle, the force drives the water against the bottom so hard that it overcomes the normal urge to flow out. This force also keeps you in your seat on a roller coaster.

Uphill flow

Did you know that it is possible to empty the liquid from one jar into another without pouring it? It's simple really. You'll need some plastic tubing. Then all you have to do is make the water flow uphill.

Fill a jar full of liquid, put a tube into it, and suck. Just before the liquid reaches your mouth, hold your thumb over the end.

Put the tube into the empty jar and hold the full jar up above the empty one. Let go with your thumb. What happens to the liquid?

The colors of the rainbow are always in the same order; red, orange, yellow, green, blue, indigo, and violet.

Making rainbows

You don't need rain to make a rainbow, you can create your very own in your backyard. Turn your back to the sun with your shadow straight ahead. Aim the hose so that the spray lands on the far side of the shadow. Do you see a perfect rainbow of color?

Siphon science

A siphon makes use of the fact that water can't help but flow from a high place to a low place. The pressure of the water in the high jar is strong enough to push water up the tube and over into the lower jar. Siphons are often used to clean fish tanks gently without disturbing the fish.

Make sure the end of the tube remains in the liquid.

Use your favorite drink in case it goes into your mouth by mistake.

The liquid flows from the full jar into the empty one, but to make this journey it has to climb uphill in part of the tube then down into the empty jar to fill it. How does this happen?

Rainbow science

Sunlight is made up of seven colors, which you normally don't see. As sunlight shines through droplets of water it bends a little. Each color bends at a slightly different angle and fans out to make a colorful arc of light called a rainbow.

Chopping Mad

Sob story

Cut an onion and what happens? You burst into tears. But why? This experiment explains the whole blubbery mystery.

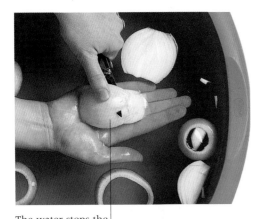

The water stops the onion "gas" from getting to you.

SCIENTISTS LOVE THE CHEMISTRY of food. Aside from helping them to discover the secrets of plants, it also allows them to nibble on some of their experiments if they ever need a snack.

The next time an adult is preparing some onions ask if you can get in on the act. First get them to peel an onion under water. Have a sniff around and you should stay dry-eyed. Then get them to chop some onions up on a board and have a good smell. It will probably set your eyes watering.

Don't touch the onions and then rub your eyes. It will only make things worse.

Sobbing science

When an onion is cut open it let's out a strong gas that turns into sulfuric acid when it mixes with air. The acid is nasty stuff and stings like crazy when it hits your eyes. Under water though, the gas is largely washed away before it gets to you. Some onions are very mild. They grow in soil that makes them sweeter, and so they do not irritate the eyes at all.

Half fill a glass container with water and add a few drops of red food coloring. Stick some celery in the colored water and leave it in a sunny place. The next day the celery leaves will be reddish – which proves they've been busy sucking up water.

Celery science

Here's how celery feeds. From the sky, sunlight hits the leaves. From the air, carbon dioxide soaks into the leaves. From the jar, water mixes with both of them. A chemical in the leaves, called chlorophyll, makes food from sunlight, carbon dioxide, and water. (The food is a kind of sugar.) In other words, celery isn't so much a hunter as a chef – it cooks up its own meals out of raw ingredients. The scientific word for this sort of food making is "photosynthesis."

Slurping celery

We use knives and forks. Creatures use fangs and claws. But how do plants tuck into their food? The reason we can't see plants feeding is because it takes place in their roots and leaves. But with the right kind of experiment you can get an idea of what's going on.

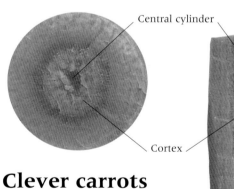

Central cylinder

Cortex

Tiny tubes in the stalk of the celery carry the water up to the leaves.

Clever carrots

Aside from being a good source of vitamins and minerals, what's so special about carrots?

Get a grown-up to cut some slices and lengths of fresh carrot. Take a good look at the patterns of circles and lines. Do you know what they are?

Carrot science

Roots pull water and minerals from the ground. The part of the carrot plant that you eat is actually the root. The dark orange "central cylinder" of a carrot contains some tubes that carry water up to the leaves, and other tubes that carry food back from the leaves to the tip of the root. The paler orange part of the carrot, the "cortex," is where the carrot stores food that it may need later.

Rain Check

THE GROUND IS COVERED IN PUDDLES, and the gutters are gurgling with water – perfect weather to study rain. Put on your raincoat, open your umbrella, and become a rain catcher. There are lots of things to discover about rainwater.

A little rain is no excuse not to take science outdoors.

Wet, wet, wet

In order to do rain experiments, you will first have to catch the rain. A rain gauge is the first step toward a working weather station (page 28). When you have trapped some rain, test it to see how acidic it is using this acid test.

To make a rain gauge, take a bucket out into the yard and place it in an open space. Stand a stick down the side of the bucket. Check every day for rain, and when you have logged it on your weather chart tip it into a jar to use for your acid rain test. Keep a record every day of the rainfall in your backyard.

Acid science

Pollution from cars and chimneys does funny things to rain. The fumes dissolve in it and turn the rain slightly acid. Acid rain eats away soft stone on many buildings, and if it's very strong it can kill trees too.

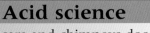

Litmus paper darken slightly in tap water.

Compare the litmus i the rainwater with th tap water and very acidic vinegar.

Litmus will go very pir in the acidic vinegar.

Record the rainfall every day for a month, then compare each day.

Here's a way to tes the kind of rain that's coming down on you Fill three jars – one wi tap water, one with rainwater, and one wit vinegar. Insert a piece litmus paper into eacl one. The pinker your litmus paper, the mor acidic the rain is.

Care for a sip?

You wouldn't gulp water from a muddy puddle (unless you were dying of thirst) because you wouldn't know if it was OK to drink. But tap water starts out as rain on the ground. So how does it end up clean to drink? The answer is a water filter. This basic filter works in the same way as the ones that give you clean tap water.

On an island in Hawaii it rains about 350 days per year!

Carefully pour the puddle water into the flowerpot. The gravel traps the large pieces of dirt floating in the water, the sand catches small pieces, and the blotting paper traps the finest specks of dirt. Compare the water seeping out of the bottom to the puddle water. Don't drink it, however. It may be clearer but it's not yet pure.

Make sure that the blotting paper covers the whole of the bottom of the flowerpot.

Line the bottom of a flowerpot with blotting paper. Fill the pot half full with fine sand and then fill it to the top with gravel. Place the flowerpot onto a jar. Take some dirty rainwater from a puddle and stir it.

Find some really dirty puddle water to filter.

Rain science

So how does rainwater get so clean by the time it runs out of our faucets? Here's how.

The rainwater makes its way into a reservoir and is then sucked into pipes by huge pumps. Large objects, such as twigs, are removed at this point.

Two chemicals are added to the water. They make specks of dirt cling together so that they sink.

The water flows into a sedimentation tank where the dirt forms a sludge at the bottom. The sludge is then removed.

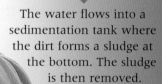

Now the water is filtered, through sand and gravel, just like your water filter to get rid of the last little bits of dirt. And it's ready to drink.

On the Move

FORCE IS REALLY IMPORTANT to scientists, and to everyone else, too. Without it no object could start or stop. See for yourself how the force of water can make things move, while the force of friction does everything it can to slow things down.

Spinning wheel

Waterwheels are machines that use the force of flowing water to do hard work. In days of old waterwheels were built beside mills to turn heavy millstones and to grind grain into flour. They have a set of blades at their rim. Flowing water collides with the blades and forces the whole wheel to spin.

You can build a test waterwheel from two plastic plates. Make a hole through the centers of both. Make the holes big enough to slide the pencil right through to become the shaft of the wheel. Get six plastic lids from aerosol cans. Use strong glue or tape to attach them to the rim of one plate, all pointing the same way.

Space the lids out equally.

Glue the second plate onto the lids. The six lids should now be clamped together as if they were inside a clamshell. Now slide the pencil through the holes to make the axle of the wheel. Hold your waterwheel under a faucet of running water.

Experiment b running the water slow and fast.

Wheel science

Waterwheels are ancient inventions – over 2,000 years old. Their "engine" is flowing water. The faster it flows, the faster the wheel spins, and the more powerful it becomes. The axle carries this power to a heavy grinding stone within.

Air power

A ball won't roll along the ground forever. That's because there's a force, called friction, which slows moving things down. Anything that rubs on something else causes friction: the ground against the ball, a brake against a wheel, and so on. But there are ways to make friction magically go away.

⚠️ **For this experiment**
use scissors to cut the top off a plastic soft drink bottle. Make a very small hole in the bottle cap. You'll need something sharp to do this, so ask an adult to give you a hand. Then blow up a large party balloon.

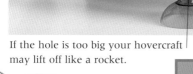

Pinch the neck of the balloon shut. Then carefully stretch the balloon mouth over the bottle cap (which is still screwed on tightly).

With the balloon in place, let go of the neck. As escaping air rushes out from under the rim of the bottle it creates a cushion of air. The bottle floats like a dream. Push it gently and watch as it glides across the table with almost no friction to stop it.

The weight of a giant hovercraft can float as smoothly as a bottle cap

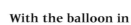
A cushion of air, like a film of oil, cuts the force of friction hugely.

If the hole is too big your hovercraft may lift off like a rocket.

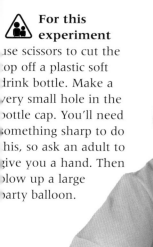

Friction science

Without a cushion of air, a hovercraft creates so much friction with the surface that even the biggest engines can't budge it. But a cushion of air reduces friction to almost nothing. That's why a few propellers can drive hundreds of tons of machinery at high speed.

Weather Report

How do they do it? Day after day TV weather forecasters look into the camera and tell us what tomorrow's weather will be like. But how can they be so sure? Or are they just guessing? Make your own weather station and keep a chart to monitor the weather.

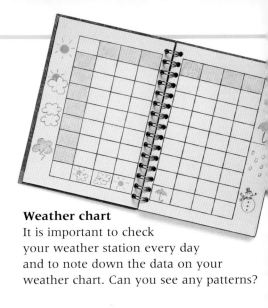

Weather chart
It is important to check your weather station every day and to note down the data on your weather chart. Can you see any patterns?

The instruments

The main pieces of equipment that you will need are a barometer to measure air pressure, a thermometer to measure temperature, a wind machine to measure wind direction and speed, and a rain gauge (see page 48) to measure the amount of rainfall.

If the pointer falls then the pressure is falling – bad weather on the way.

No weather station is complete without a thermometer. Record the temperature daily on your weather chart.

A barometer measures air pressure – the weight of air that presses down on the ground. The air pressure falls if a storm is near, and rises when fine weather is approaching. Here's how to make your own. Cut off a balloon's neck with a pair of scissors and stretch the rest over a jar. Fasten the sides down with tape. Fasten two straws together and tape one end to the center of the balloon. Stand a ruler up and measure the movement of the marker every day.

Wind machine

Weather forecasters use a wind vane to tell them the direction the wind is coming from, and an anemometer to tell them how hard it's blowing. Here's how to build the two machines in one.

On a square piece of plastic, draw an arc of 90°. Mark from 0 to 90° with a protractor at 10° intervals. Cut out a pointer and a tail and attach one at either end of a 23.5 in (60 cm) piece of bamboo.

Attach the square piece of plastic to the bamboo with tape, as shown. Take a long piece of aluminum foil and tape it to one end of a toothpick. Pierce the plastic square at the top and slide the toothpick through the hole so that the foil strip can swing freely. Tie a thick piece of wire around the center of the bamboo leaving a long prong below it. Insert the wire prong into a long piece of bamboo.

What's blowing?

Weather comes with the wind, so if the wind changes it's usually a sign that something is brewing. Weather forecasters use a vane to show them which direction the wind is coming from. To measure wind speed, note the degree the swinging strip reaches. 90° means no wind, more than 50° means stay indoors!

The swinging foil shows the wind speed.

The wire prong should allow the vane to swing around freely in the wind.

Use a compass to mark north, south, east, and west on a flowerpot base and note the wind direction.

Forecasting

So how do we predict the weather? There are over 10,000 weather stations all over the world, which send information to forecasting centers. Many stations send up balloons with instruments attached – the drift measures wind speed and direction, and the instruments hold other information. They rise to about 12-19 miles (20-30 km) then they burst dropping instruments, which fall by parachute.

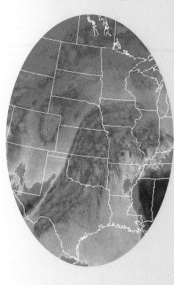

Weather satellites orbit the Earth and show pictures of the weather conditions (see below.) With all this daily information, no wonder forecasters have a good idea of tomorrow's weather.

Hot and Cold

A GREAT LAW OF SCIENCE says that if you let hot things be, they cool down by themselves. But never, ever the other way around. Like water on a hill, heat can only flow downhill. Luckily, there's a delicious way to test this law.

Salt freezer

Here's how to make ice cream the old-fashioned way using only salt, ice, and science.

Mix a tablespoon of cream with two of milk and one of chocolate powder in a small glass. Put a bed of ice cubes in a bowl and sprinkle with salt. Put the glass on top and very carefully stack layers of ice and salt all around it.

Cover the bowl with a dish towel and leave it to sit. Stir every few minutes.

After an hour, take the glass out of the bowl and taste some wonderful home-made chocolate ice cream. But how does it work? The towel stops warm air from flowing into the chilled bowl. Salt forces the ice to melt fast. The melting ice steals heat from the mixture, chilling it down until it freezes.

Buttered peas

Heat flows like traffic – sometimes fast and sometimes slow. Some things, like copper, let heat flow through them quickly – they are good conductors – and some things make a complete mess of it. They are called insulators. Which is which in this experiment?

Get a wooden spoon, a plastic spoon, a metal spoon, and a straw. Use some butter to stick a pea at the same height on each item. Place them in a pot.

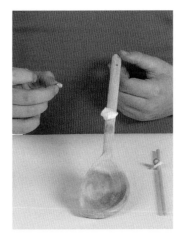

Pour some hot water into the pot. Which pea will fall first, do you think, and then in what order will the rest fall? Which is the best insulator? Which makes the best conductor?

If you want to change the taste, try a drop or two of vanilla flavoring instead of chocolate.

Conducting science

Every single thing in the Universe is made up of tiny particles called atoms. If one end of a conductor heats up, the atoms inside it start to jiggle around like hot popcorn in a pan. They whack their neighbors and make these atoms jostle too. Like this, heat shuffles along from atom to atom, until the whole conductor is hot. Metal is a good conductor, which is why it is often used to make saucepans.

The coldest it can ever be is about minus 459°F (273°C)

Hot spot

If there's no place for heat to flow away, then whatever it's in stays hot. That's why a hot drink in a thermos flask stays hot all day. Here's how to test this.

Wrap and tape two layers of aluminum foil around a small jar (shiny side facing in). Pour warm water into the jar and screw on the lid.

Put a cork in the bottom of a big jar. Stand the small jar on it and screw on the lid. The water should stay warm for ages since it's so hard for the heat to escape.

Shadow Catching

ON A FRESH MORNING, as the sunlight plays among the trees, shadows dapple the ground wherever you look. It's perfect weather for proving that the Sun is a clock and also that the Earth is moving.

Shadow time

It's time to prove that we can tell the time by using the Sun. Stand a stick in a flowerpot in a sunny area. Every hour mark where the stick's shadow falls using a small flowerpot with the time written on it. The next day the shadows fall at the same time. The sun measures time very well – as long as we know how to read it.

Ray ban
Sunlight travels in straight lines called "rays." When rays hit something solid they get blocked. On the far side of the tree where sunlight can't reach, a patch of "no rays" forms – a shadow.

By using these shadows, you will find you have a timepiece!

Shadow science

The Earth spins around once every 24 hours, which means that at any time half the Earth faces the Sun and enjoys daylight (day) and half is in shadow (night). As the Sun seems to move from east to west the shadows it casts appear to move too. But actually it's us that moves, not the Sun.

When did we learn to tell the time?
It took thousands of years to figure out that the Earth did a twirl in 24 hours. The Babylonians were the first to work it out 4,000 years ago by watching the Sun travel across the sky. They made the first sundials – a sundial has a pointer called a gnomon, and the gnomon's shadow shows the time on a flat dial marked in hours.

The gnomon's shadow points to the time.

Galloping shadows

Shadows shrink and grow throughout the day. They are at their biggest in the morning and again in the evening. Prove this by standing in exactly the same spot several times during the day.
Each time, get a friend to mark the tip of your shadow with a stick. When is your shadow the longest, or shortest?

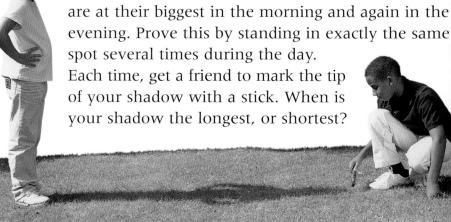

The biggest shadow
in the world is a
solar eclipse

Diamond ring

One of the most spectacular moments in a solar eclipse is what is known as the "diamond ring effect." This happens as the last sunlight shines through valleys on the Moon. It produces a stunning, bright spot at the edge of the Moon that only lasts a few seconds.

The ultimate shadow

The biggest shadow you can ever hope to see is the shadow of the Moon as it falls across the surface of the Earth. This is an eclipse of the Sun. From the ground it looks like the Sun is being eaten away by the Moon until it is completely hidden.

The Sun is hidden by the Moon.

An eclipse forms when the Sun, Earth, and Moon line up so that the Moon lies between us and the Sun. Then the shadow of the Moon sweeps over the Earth. If the eclipse is total, it turns day into night for a few minutes. If you were an astronaut hanging around out in space, this is what you would see. A big shadow where the Moon partly hides the Sun (a partial eclipse) and a smaller, darker shadow where it blocks all of the Sun (total eclipse).

The light from the Sun travels toward the Earth as if on a normal sunny day.

The Moon moves between the Sun and the Earth.

The Moon's shadow causes a total eclipse on one part of the Earth.

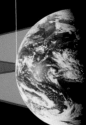

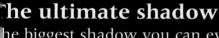

Farming Crystals

HERE'S A USEFUL LAW OF NATURE: "If it isn't alive then it's probably a crystal." That's because just about every nonliving thing you can bump into is made of crystals, including rocks, metals, snowflakes, beaches, and even salt and sugar.

Crystal science

All crystals have very regular shapes with flat surfaces and sharp edges. Many look like little boxes. It's all because their atoms are bolted together in orderly, geometric shapes. Usually you need a microscope to see them.

Field of crystals

You need a watery solution to grow crystals. This one uses Epsom salts, because they make such wonderful spiky shapes.

Stir a tablespoon of Epsom salts into five tablespoons of warm water until it's all dissolved. Then gently pour the solution into a dark-colored shallow dish and place it in the sun.

As the water evaporates you'll see crop of white crystal needles start grow in the dish. They are Epso salt crystals (or hydrated magnesiu sulfate, as chemists would say Make sure you wash your hand when you finish this experimen

Grow a crystal

Growing crystals takes time. You won't need fertilizer, but you will have to "seed" crystals by growing them in a salty solution.

The small crystal acts as a seed. After a few weeks a very much larger crystal grows around it as the water in the jar evaporates.

Make a salty solution by dissolving as much salt as you can in a jar of warm water. Pour a little of the solution into a shallow dish. Let it evaporate for a week. Then pick out the biggest crystal you can and tie some thread to it. Dangle the crystal from a pencil into the jar of solution.

Crystal icicles

Over thousands of years, dripping water leaves great columns of minerals in caves. Those that cling tightly to the roof are called "stalactites." But if they sit, tightly, on the cave floor then they're called "stalagmites." Here's how to grow a crystal icicle – a stalactite – without having to go caving or wait 1,000 years. This one takes about a week to grow.

Stalactite science

Water dissolves limestone as it seeps through the ground. As it drips from the roof of a cave it leaves behind a thin crust of limestone minerals. Slowly, very slowly, the crust grows into a long stalactite.

Fill two jars with warm water. Add baking soda and stir until you can't dissolve any more.

Take a length of thick yarn and attach a paper clip to each end. Lower the ends of the yarn into a jar so that it is suspended between the two. Place a dish under the lowest part of the yarn to catch the drips. Let the experiment sit for several days.

Quartz is the most common crystal of all

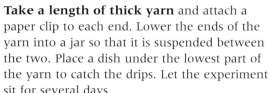

The solution of baking soda soaks the yarn and when it gets to the lowest point of the yarn it drips. Each drip leaves a little soda behind. Drip by drip, the soda crystals grow. After a few days you'll have a white stalactite hanging from the yarn.

You might even get a stalagmite growing up from the dish.

⚠ Soil Science

IT MAKES YOU DIRTY. It gets you mucky. And a single spoonful of it would taste disgusting. Yet without it we would all starve. "It" is soil – the stuff from which our vegetables, our fruit, and even our meat (in a roundabout way) comes. But what exactly is soil?

Crawling under your feet

Soil is crawling with thousands of creatures. Animals, such as moles and worms, appear above ground every so often and are large enough to spot. Here's how to meet some of the tiny creatures you rarely see. Take handfuls of soil from different parts of your backyard.

A small patch of soil holds millions of worms, insects, grubs, and fungi.

Rest a funnel in a jar. Put a handful of soil in a sieve and put it in the funnel. Bend a lamp close over the soil and leave it for about half an hour. The little creatures in the soil are not used to light and will burrow away from it until they drop out of the funnel into the jar. Tip the creatures into a saucer and, using a magnifying glass, study them close up. (Do not leave them under the light for too long – they might overheat.)

How many different types of animals appear in your jar?

Make a record of the ones you find. Try to identify them later.

Something rotten

Nature doesn't waste a thing. As soon as a plant or animal dies it rots, or decays. Slice a red pepper, or any other fruit or vegetable, in half. Place it on a dish, and day by day watch what takes place. What does it look like after two weeks?

Rotten science

The living organisms in the soil are nature's recyclers. They include bacteria, fungi, and various animals. Their job is to break down dead organic material (plants and animals) and let the nutrients they contain back into the soil so that other plants grow healthily. Worms are very good recyclers – find out how by turning the page.

What's in it?

Soil is a mixture of all sorts of things. We know that it contains living organisms and decaying plants and animals, but what else is there? Gather soil samples from your backyard and put them into jars. Add water so that the jars are nearly full. Shake well then let them stand.

Rotten plants and animals (organic matter) float at the top of the water, and rocks and minerals sink. Rock fragments will sink first, sandy pieces will settle as the next layer. Fine clay sinks slowly and sits on the sand.

Soil from different areas will contain varying amounts of minerals and organic matter.

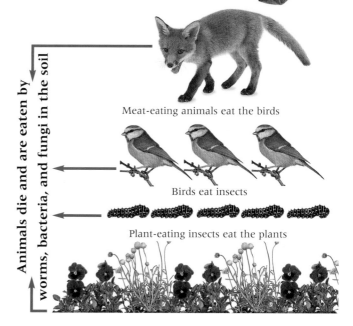

Animals die and are eaten by worms, bacteria, and fungi in the soil

Meat-eating animals eat the birds

Birds eat insects

Plant-eating insects eat the plants

Say hello to dinner

Every plant and animal in the world is dinner for something else. Even human beings, after they die and are buried, end up as meals for worms and bacteria. The route from one stomach to the next is called a food chain. There are many kinds of food chains. Take a look at the simple one above.

Wet, Wet, Wet

WATER IS PRETTY IMPORTANT in the kitchen, but have you ever thought about the changes it goes through every day? Heat it up or cool it down, and some rather weird things start to happen.

Makes a change

For this experiment you hardly have to do a thing, just hang around the kitchen and you'll see how water goes through some pretty amazing transformations.

Heat up water enough and it turns into a gas called steam. The steam escapes into the air where it mixes with clouds and other moisture.

Steam

Watch the drips of a leaky faucet. This is the liquid state in which we see water most often, although it only looks like this between a temperature of 32°F (0°C) and 212°F (100°C).

Water

Look in the freezer. It's 5°F (-15°C) or colder in there. At this temperature water turns to solid ice. That's why the Arctic Ocean has an ice lid on it for much of the year.

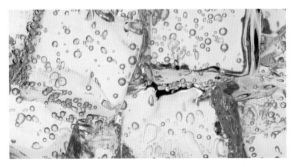

Ice

Light at the top

Did you know warm water is lighter than cold water? So if hot water weighs a tiny bit less than cold, does it float on top? You may get soaked with this experiment, but at least you'll get an answer.

⚠ **Find two jars** exactly the same size. Fill one with hot water and add a drop of red food coloring. Fill the other with cold water and add blue food coloring. Fill up the jars until the water bulges over the rim.

Watery science

Hot water is less dense than cold water, so it floats on top of it. That's because less dense things float on more dense ones. Lighter warm water always rises to the top of cold dense water. This is especially important in the sea since it helps currents to flow around the world.

Gently place a square piece of cardboard over the red jar so it seals in the water. Now you have to act quickly. Pick up the red jar and flip it upside down. If you get it right, the water will hold the cardboard in place. If you don't – you'll get soaked.

You may have to practice flipping the top jar a few times.

Put the red jar exactly on top of the blue jar. Hold them together and get someone to ease the cardboard out carefully. What happens? Try the same experiment, but with the blue jar on top. What happens to the colors this time?

⚠️🦋 Worm Farm

EVERYBODY LOVES WORMS. Gardeners like them because they make gardens healthy. Birds like them as a tasty meal. And once you understand what an amazing job they do, you'll start to enjoy them too.

Home from home

A worm farm gives us the chance to find out what happens underground. Fill a bowl with alternate layers of soil and sand. Put some leaves and veggies on the top. Add water to make the soil damp and let some worms make themselves at home.

Charmed, I'm sure

Worm charming is a great way to watch worms. Pretend to be a shower of rain by jumping up and down. The worms will come to the surface to enjoy the drops.

Fallen leaves   Soil   Fine sand

Keep the worm farm somewhere cool and dark.

Heads or tails?

One way not to tell the head of a worm from the tail is by listening to which end snores. It's actually very hard to tell. Luckily there's a simple way to find out. Place a worm in a dish and touch one end very gently. The worm shrinks back. Now touch the other end; it shrinks back too but the end that shrinks the quickest is the tail.

Worms have sensitive tails that pull back rapidly if touched. This is an escape reaction in case a bird tries to grab on before they can hide.

The saddle – the thick part that carries the eggs.

Worm walk

Look closely at an earthworm. You will notice that it is divided into segments – muscles. The worm also has a long muscle running right through its body. To move, the worm contracts the segments and stretches its body muscle forward. Tiny bristles help it grip the soil. Next the worm contracts its long muscle and draws up the rest of the body behind the front section so moving forward.

Worm science

Earthworms are vital to the soil. On the surface they eat decaying plants and animals and then, as they move through the soil, the food passes through the worm and is deposited behind it in the tunnels it digs. This mixes the soil up and distributes the nutrients from above. The tunnels also let the soil breathe and help rainwater to drain away.

Without earthworms, the soil would become hard and airless.

Check every day, and you'll soon see tunnels as worms eat through the soil. The layers of soil will start to mix, and leaves will be pulled into the tunnels. After the project, put the worms back where you found them.

Worm secrets

• Worms have no bones. They are bendable and squishy and have skin you can see through.

• There are over 1,800 species of earthworms in the world.

• One Australian species of earthworm can grow as long as 11 ft (3.3 m). That's the size of two humans lying lengthwise.

Under Pressure

NOTHING MAKES WATER HAPPIER than when it's flowing downhill. All it needs is a clear channel and enough pressure to send it on its way. From then on it just flows until it reaches the lowest level it can find.

Juicy siphon

A siphon is a pump that runs on natural pressure and nothing else. That's why it can only flow one way – from a higher level to a lower one.

Fill a pitcher with juice and dip the end of a clean tube into it. Suck on the other end of the tube until juice nears your lips. Then quickly cap the tube with your thumb.

Once you get the juice flowing it won't want to stop.

Siphon science

As liquid flows down the long side of a siphon, it draws up more on the short side. If the long side ends lower down than the short side, the liquid keeps on flowing. Siphons have a gentle sucking action – this is why they are used in toilet tanks and to drain gas tanks.

Move from glass to glass so each gets a fair share of juice.

Put the capped end of the tube in a glass and take your finger away. Juice will flow up out of the pitcher and down into the glass. Keep the pitcher higher so the juice always runs downhill.

Fountain attack

With this science trick, offer victims a drink of water (even though it will never end up in their mouth). Fill a plastic bottle right to the top with water. Put the cap on tightly. Lay the bottle on its side and make a small hole about half way down with a pen.

If you are feeling extra wicked, get your victim to make the hole without telling him why.

Hold the bottle with the hole pointing at your victim. Ask if he wants a drink of water. Water won't flow out of the hole while the cap is on because no air can get in at the top. Then unscrew the cap and watch as a jet of water shoots out.

The lower the hole in the bottle, the more water pressure there is above it and the further the fountain will splash.

Well blow me down!

Use an old law of science to trick your friends. Bet them that you can lift a ball up simply by blowing on it. They'll never believe you can do it, until they see it with their own eyes.

Make a small yogurt cup and make a hole in the bottom. Feed a straw through and seal it in place with modeling clay.

Blowing science

What happens is this: as air speeds up its pressure drops so much that nearby air rushes in to fill the gap. When you blow in-rushing air tries desperatcly to get up into the cup. The ball is in the way of the air, so it gets pushed up into the cup – even though you are still blowing with all your might.

Place the cup over a table tennis ball and blow hard (don't suck). The ball will rise into the cup and spin as if you were sucking as hard as a vacuum cleaner.

⚠ On Tap

FOR ANIMALS, A POND in the garden is like us having faucets in the bathroom. It means a regular supply of water to drink and water to have a bath in. Even a minipond is a magnet for wildlife. All you need is a quiet corner of your backyard that gets a little sun.

If you spot a creature lurking in the pondweed, scoop it gently into a jar of water (return it carefully when you have finished studying it).

⚠ Minipond

To make your own minipond you will need some real pond water. Go to a pond near you and, with an adult, collect some water in a bowl. Dig a hole in your yard and lower the bowl until the rim is level with the ground. Add some pondweed (from a local nursery) and some stones and pebbles so that the water animals have somewhere to hide.

Pond science

Pond water is already full of all sorts of goodies that your visitors will like, but tap water will do just as well. Plants are essential in a pond as they supply oxygen and keep the water fresh. Keep the pond filled up in hot weather.

Draw the animals in as much detail as you can.

Feel the tension

Here is an experiment to show that insects can walk on water. Simply fill a glass with water and drop a matchstick onto it. Surface tension lets the match rest on top of the surface. It doesn't even get wet!

Surface science

Now and then you may see water spiders skittering across your pond. They are so light that they can sit on water without sinking into it. They make use of a special force called surface tension. It pulls the surface of water together so much that it forms a stretchy skin. Surface tension is why raindrops are round and why water spiders glide about without getting wet. Sadly, it's not strong enough to hold up humans.

Pond logbook

Keep a pond logbook. As the days go by, all kinds of small insects will visit. Some, like damselflies, may even lay their eggs in it. Snails and frogs may come to it, and birds will drink from it.

Dragonflies, like minihelicopters, can hover, dart backward, make 90° turns, and come to an instant stop.

Frogs can breathe through their skin as well as their nostrils.

Flying dragons

Look out for dragonflies that lay their eggs in ponds, and watch them fly at lightning speed – a dragonfly's wings flap about 20 times a second.

arge clumps of ogspawn float ear the surface nd are easy find.

Frog march

Here's something to watch out for in ponds. In spring, frogs lay huge amounts of frogspawn. Look in your pond, or a local pond, for the jellylike eggs. Watch them, and within two or three weeks the eggs will turn into tadpoles and then into frogs. If you are lucky enough to find some eggs, keep a log of their growth.

Hairy lightning

This experiment makes one of the tiniest bolts of lightning you'll ever see. It's an example of static electricity – the kind of charge that happens when two things rub together.

Cut a piece from a Styrofoam tray so you end up with a bent corner.

Lightning makes a supersonic shock wave that we call thunder

Tape the bent section to the center of an aluminum pie pan to form a handle. Now rub the rest of the tray quickly across your hair.

Set the tray upside down on a table. Using the handle ONLY, pick up the pie pan and drop it onto the tray. Very slowly touch the pie pan with the tip of a finger. Watch how a spark flies! Do this in the dark if you want colored lightning.

Creating Currents

WHY ARE THUNDERSTORMS like combing your hair? Because both can create lightning. The sort on your head is just a crackle, but the bolts that zap between clouds are five times hotter than the surface of the sun.

Sparky science

Rubbing the tray on your hair piles up an electric charge on it. The pie pan pulls some of the charge off the tray. As you touch it, the charge surges toward you as a spark. When the same kind of thing happens in clouds it creates lightning.

Pepper un-shaker

You can separate salt from fine-ground pepper two ways: very slowly with your fingers or quickly by letting static electricity do the hard work. The trick is that pepper weighs a lot less than salt.

Both pepper and salt are attracted. But because the pepper is lighter it leaps up first. If you lower the pen too much you'll get the salt sticking too.

prinkle a pinch of salt and pepper onto plate. Now rub a pen very hard with a oolen cloth so it collects a charge. Wave e pen slowly over the plate, and the epper jumps up and sticks to it. The alt stays behind.

Water power

Not even water can resist the harms of electricity. With his experiment you can se static electricity to bend vater flowing from a faucet.

ub a balloon hard on your hair. nen hold it close to a thin stream flowing water. The flow bends as is attracted by the static on the lloon. How attractive are you? ub a few balloons on your hair d then stick them to yourself to d out.

Attractive Greeks

Static electricity was first investigated in ancient Greece about 2,600 years ago. A Greek philosopher called Thales found that when he rubbed amber (a honey-colored fossilized resin) with cloth he could attract pieces of straw to it. The Greeks called amber *elektron* and from it we get our word *electricity*.

Striking lightning

A bolt of lightning is created when water droplets and ice crystals in clouds are whirled together so hard they become charged with static electricity. Opposite charges collect at the top and bottom of a cloud until the attraction between them is so great that a bolt of lightning leaps between the two (like the spark from your finger to the pie pan).

Look up it. Try to guess how tall and how old it is. Then read on and see how accurate you were!

Tree of Life

THEY ARE ALL AROUND US and stretch high above us. But ask a simple question about trees, like how old they are, and people are stumped! Here's how to measure a tree's size and figure out how old it is.

How tall?

Measuring a tree is a little harder than measuring a human. You can't just pick it up and measure it against a wall. It is, however, much easier than you imagine. All you need is a stick, a long piece of string, a steady hand, and a friend.

Position a friend at the bottom of the tree. Stand a good distance back and hold a stick out straight in front of you. Make your thumb level with the bottom of the tree and the top of the stick level with the crown.

Happy birthday to yew!

You can roughly work out the age of a tree by measuring around the trunk, about 60 in (150 cm) above the ground. Divide the answer by 1 in (2.5 cm) to find the approximate age. Some trees are not suitable experiments – for example, yew and redwood.

Sap alert

Trees have sap inside that runs all the way up to the top. Trees like pines have a special, sticky sap. It flows out of cuts in order to keep off bugs and other animals while the wound heals and new bark grows over it.

How big?

The California redwoods are the tallest trees in the world. Their trunks can grow up to 25 ft (7.5 m) wide. From base to towering top they can reach a staggering 278 ft (85 m).

Growing old

Bristlecone pines in California are the oldest trees in the world. Some have been around for over 4,000 years – they were in their prime when the Pharaohs ruled Egypt. Imagine what they could tell us if they had memories.

Try to track down the tallest tree in your neighborhood.

Keeping your thumb very still, swivel the stick sideways until it is level with the ground. Ask your friend to walk away from the tree and stand at the end of the stick. Go over and give them an end of string. Run the string back to the base of the tree, measure it, and there you have it – the height.

The most accurate way to tell a tree's age is to count rings. A tree adds one ring each year.

There's only one way to find the age of a tree that's 100% accurate – unfortunately it involves chopping it down!

Hard and Soft

THINK OF SOMETHING HARD? No, not math – just something that's hard when you touch it. Now guess what happens if you heat it or freeze it? Many things go through near-magical changes if we play around with their temperature.

Put your piece of the chocolate in the fridge.

Getting warmer

Play a chocolatey trick on a friend. Put a slab of chocolate in the fridge overnight. Leave another piece somewhere warm. Next day put the two pieces out ready to be eaten. Pick up your rock hard piece and have a bite. It may be almost impossible to take a nibble. Then offer the other piece to your friend. But be careful, things might get a little sticky.

Melting science

Everything goes soupy if you heat it enough. This temperature is called its melting point. For example ice melts at 32°F (0°C), and lead melts at 622°F (328°C). But you have to heat iron up to 2,802°F (1,539°C) before it melts.

It may have melted, but it's still chocolate!

Cold chocolate is so hard it clanks against the plate.

⚠ Getting harder

Pick up a piece of bread and feel how soft and squeezy it is. Now put a couple of slices in the toaster and let them cook. Once they pop up, and cool, what do you notice first? Of course – toast is harder and crunchier than untoasted bread and a lot drier too.

Toast is just a nice sounding word for slightly burned bread. As bread roasts it forms a layer of ash (the brown and black specks) just the same as wood and paper do in a fire. Meanwhile, the moisture that made the bread soft evaporates to leave a warm toasty texture that's delicious with butter and honey.

Heat makes some things
go harder and others go softer

⚠ Getting solid

A fresh egg is runny and floppy. But after boiling it in water (get help with this) for a few minutes the white goes hard. The yolk stays runny. Boil it a little longer and the yolk hardens too. So heat sometimes makes things go from liquid to solid.

Getting wetter

Hold an ice cube in your hands for a few minutes. It starts out dry, but soon it gets very wet. That's because ice goes from solid to liquid as it gets warmer.

Toasty science

When a slice of bread is toasted, it starts to burn. Burning is a chemical reaction during which oxygen in the air reacts with chemicals in the bread to give off heat and smoke, and to leave behind dark black ash.

Juice, rocks, air

Apple juice is liquid, rocks are solid, and air is gassy. In fact every single substance in the world is one of these three: a gas, a liquid, or a solid. This trio is also called "The Three States of Matter." Under the right conditions, apple juice can turn into a solid or a gas. Stick some in the freezer overnight and it will be in a rock hard state by morning. Boil it up in a pot and it will turn into a gas (steam) and evaporate into the air.

Any substance you name can change from one state to another. Solid rock will turn into a liquid if you heat it enough. Just visit an active volcano to see rocks flowing like honey. And if you take a bottle of air and chill it in outer space you'd see it turn into an icy liquid.

Move it!

GARDENING CAN BE BACK-BREAKING work. But thanks to levers you have no excuse because they make lots of tiring jobs so much easier. They change a little effort from you into enough power to haul a great big, heavy load.

What a drag!
When you've been gardening and you have a full sack of garbage, you'll find it pretty hard to lift. You may just be able to drag it across the yard, but don't overdo it. Help is at hand.

Think about how the wheelbarrow works to help you move this load.

Levers make light work of some really heavy backyard tasks

Now put the load into a wheelbarrow and trundle it to the other end of the garden. Easier? How long does it take you to get it across now? The wheelbarrow is one of the most useful garden levers. It's a machine that seems to give you extra strength. That's what levers are all about – turning you into a superkid.

Wheelbarrow races

The trick with a lever is to get exactly the right balance between the fulcrum, load, and effort to make the load lightest. Have a wheelbarrow race with your friends and find out where to put your "load" so that you can move fastest.

Try putting your friend near to the handle end of the wheelbarrow. The load (your friend) is nearer the effort (you) so you will find that she is difficult to lift – it's quite a struggle.

Now place her at the other end – over the fulcrum. Now that the fulcrum is taking most of her weight, the wheelbarrow is easier to push. You'll probably win the race.

Lever science

Here comes the science part. All levers move up and down around a point called a "fulcrum." With it, the lever raises and lowers the "load." The force that does all the hard work of shifting the load is the "effort." And that, in a nutshell, is levers. On the wheelbarrow, the wheel acts as the fulcrum. The load is the sack, and your grip on the handles is the effort. The wheelbarrow is a good lever so makes light work of a job.

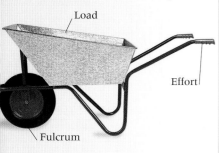
Load
Effort
Fulcrum

ow on earth can ou move such heavy object ore easily?

Lever power

You are pedaling at full speed down a hill, and a cat strays in front of you. You slam on the brakes and stop instantly. Wow – talk about finger power! It's all due to the levers that sit between your fingers and the wheels. (The brake handle is a lever, and both brake arms are levers too.) They multiply your strength until it can stop your weight, the bike's weight, and the speed of both in the space of just a few yards.

Everyday levers

Did you know that parts of your body are levers too? Take your foot. When you take a step, the ball of your foot becomes the fulcrum, the load is your body weight, and the effort that moves is in all your leg muscles. Try to think of other levers that you use every day. From little levers – nail clippers and nutcrackers – to larger levers – garden shears and scales – to massive levers like huge diggers.

Light Fantastic

LIGHT IS PRETTY USEFUL STUFF. Without it, you couldn't read the words on this page or see the faces of your friends. When you bend light it can make things look bigger, and sometimes it splits into different colors to make a rainbow.

Color detective

Many colors are not true colors. Instead they are mixed from other colors. Here's an experiment that separates the true from the mixed.

Get some candy-covered chocolates and pick out three different colors. Put a few of each color in a saucer and add some water. Turn them over so that the color comes off and mixes with the water. Cut some coffee filters into strips, and put one in each of the saucers with one end in the water. As the colors move up the filters the mixed ones start to separate.

Color science

Light comes in waves of different lengths and our eyes see each length as a color. The shortest waves that we can detect are violet. Thereafter they lengthen into blue and green, then yellow and red. The longest visible light waves are a deep red color.

Gelatin glasses

Did you know you can make a magnifying glass out of a dessert? It's not hard – especially if you like the taste of fruit gelatin.

Get a large pack of gelatin dessert. Lemon or any pale color works best. Get a grown-up to boil 7 fl oz (200 ml) of water and to put it in a pitcher. Dump the "raw" gelatin into the bowl and carefully pour the water onto it. Stir until the gelatin has dissolved.

After the mixture cools, put some in a ladle. You can also use soup spoons or large measuring spoons. Carefully set the spoon on a dish. Put it in the fridge.

Magnifying science

The gelatin mold forms a curved lens that bends light rays – just like a magnifying glass. Light rays pass through it and spread out. They form an image that appears to be bigger than the words or pictures you were originally looking at.

Fake rainbow

You can make colors appear in clear plastic, but you'll need a pair of polaroid sunglasses. Shine a bright light at a cassette box and then look at it through a pair of sunglasses. You should see a rainbow effect made up of bright colors. The polaroid sunglasses cut out some of the colors that make up white light, and you see the colors that are left.

Four hours later the mold ought to be set. Turn the spoon out onto a wet, clear plate. If you are using smaller spoons you can turn them out onto some clear plastic, like a cassette case lid. Run hot water over the back of the spoons to free the sticky gelatin.

Glasses were first worn 700 years ago in Europe

The curved surface of the gelatin mold makes beams of light bend so that they magnify things.

Hold the gelatin blob over some words or pictures, and you'll see you have a lens that magnifies them. Two small blobs of gelatin give you gelatin glasses!

Rainbow science

Real rainbows happen after clouds start to clear and sunlight strikes raindrops that are still falling. The light bends and travels onward to your eye, so that you see it split into many colors.

Fast Brains

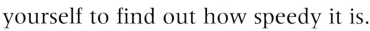

DID YOU KNOW THAT YOUR BRAIN is lightning quick? It can sense and react to something faster than you can say "ouch." Test yourself to find out how speedy it is.

Mark the ground with a rope and stand with your arms out – easy!

Wobble test

Toddlers fall over all the time. Why don't you? Because as you grow up, your brain learns what to do if the ground slopes suddenly – and you develop a sense of balance. Try this trick if you've forgotten what it's like to wobble like a toddler.

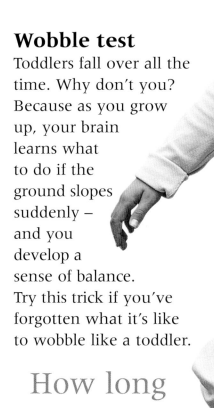

How long can you stay upright on one foot?

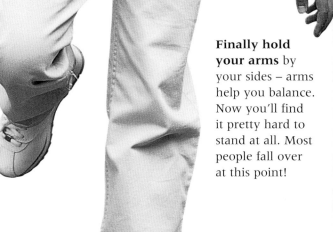

Now lift a foot. This halves the balance information that the feet send to the brain. Are you still steady?

Finally hold your arms by your sides – arms help you balance. Now you'll find it pretty hard to stand at all. Most people fall over at this point!

Ask a friend to blindfold you. Now your eyes can't tell your brain where the ground is. You'll be wobbling hard!

Eye ball

Sometimes your hands are so quick they seem to have a mind of their own – like when they catch a flying ball. Throw a ball into the air and catch it – fairly easy. Now do it with your eyes closed – bonk!

Why is it hard to catch with eyes shut? Because your brain has no idea where your hands are supposed to be.

Quick reaction

Test the speed of your brain's reactions with this simple game. Tie four colored pieces of tape around a stick and ask a friend to hold it just above your hand. Get him to drop it without warning while you snap your fingers shut as quickly as possible to catch it. What color did you grab near? The nearer your finger was to the bottom, the faster your brain worked. Can you train your brain to speed up by practicing?

Signals are flashed back and forth to your brain at up to 330 ft (100 m) per second

Body science

So why does your body know how to remain steady and upright all the time (well, almost all the time)? Or how do you catch a ball when it is thrown to you?

Well, your brain has an image of your body and knows what position your arms, legs, trunk, and head must be in to remain upright. Senses in parts of the body, such as in the eyes, muscles, ears, and skin send high-speed messages to the brain through nerve branches.

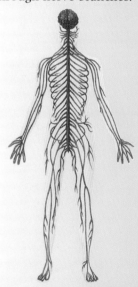

If any of these senses are taken away, your brain doesn't get all the information it needs, and your body will not behave correctly. In the wobble test, your brain only has one leg on the ground so it uses your arms and eyes to balance. Your eyes are then subtracted and lastly your arms. Now your brain has too little information to keep you upright. In the ball test, the most vital sense – the eyes – is taken away.

Making Sense

HUMAN BEINGS HAVE FIVE SENSES: smell, taste, sight, hearing, and touch. Smell and taste are really important because without them there would be no point in having fantastic inventions like pizza and ice cream!

Half fill four egg cups with water. Squeeze some lemon juice into one, add two teaspoons of sugar to the next, two teaspoons of salt to the third, and some tonic water to the last one.

Tongue map

The surface of your tongue has hundreds of tiny taste buds for telling the difference between "yum!" and "yuck!" Here's an experiment to find out what your tongue can do.

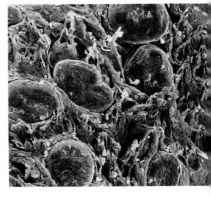

Budding talent
What we taste is all down to special taste buds. They are dotted among thousands of tiny bumps that coat the surface of the tongue. Nerve-endings in the taste buds sense a flavor and send a message about it to the brain.

Dab your tongue with paper towel before you taste from each egg cup.

The center
of your tongue
can't taste
much at all

Use a cotton swab to try each mixture. Touch it to the middle, sides, and back of your tongue. Which parts of your tongue are best at sensing salty, sweet, sour, and bitter flavors?

Blind tasting

Strangely, when it comes to tasting, your nose is just as important as your tongue. That's why, when you are all stopped up with a cold, food seems to lose its flavor. Here's a way to prove it.

Pour three different fruit juices into three glasses. Get a friend to blindfold you with a scarf and then taste each glass in turn.

Rinse your mouth out with water between tastings so it doesn't get too confused.

Smelly science

We smell things at the very top of our nose, where there are two postage-stamp-sized patches of about 10 million "smell" cells. When a smell bumps into these cells they send a message to the brain, which has a brilliant memory for figuring out smells.

Get touchy

Can you rely on your sense of touch to let you know when things are hot and cold? Try this experiment to find out. Get three glasses and fill one with hot water. Fill another with cold water and ice. Put a mixture of hot and cold water in the third glass. Put one finger in the hot water and another in the cold. Leave them for a minute.

Dip the hot finger into the warm water. The warm water will feel cold because it's not as hot as your finger. Try dipping the cold finger into the warm water. The water should feel hot. This is because you can only feel if something is hotter or colder than your skin.

Tasty science

Although you can identify hundreds of kinds of food, your tongue only knows about four tastes: sweet, sour, salty, or bitter. Most taste buds are on the edges and back of your tongue.

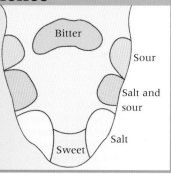

Bitter

Sour

Salt and sour

Salt

Sweet

Now pinch your nose shut and do it again. How hard is it to tell one juice from another? Nose open – it's easy to tell one fruit flavor from another. Nose shut – smell turned off – and the juices all have the same dull flavor.

Heartbeat

YOUR HEART IS THE STRONGEST thing in your whole body. It pumps all day and all night for a lifetime without stopping. Put your heart and lungs to the test and find out how strong your body is.

Heart work

When your heart beats, it sends a wave of blood through your body – this is called a pulse. If you are active, the pulse beats faster and your lungs work harder so you breathe faster too. Measure your heartrate and breaths after exercise to see out how much more work they do.

Before you exercise, time with a stopwatch how often you breathe in one minute. Next count your pulse rate for a minute. Find your pulse by holding your forefinger and middle finger on your wrist. The average for a 10-year-old is 80 beats per minute.

Now go and do some vigorous exercise.

Right after exercise, check your breathing rate. Count how many breathes your lungs take in a minute. How many more breathes do your lungs need now compared to before?

Time a minute while you count your pulse. How much faster is it? Now time how long your breathing and pulse rates take to return to normal. The quicker they recover, the fitter you are.

The heart of the matter

You know how many times your heart beats per minute, but have you ever thought about how hard it works to pump blood all around your body? Fill one bowl with water and place an empty one next to it. Use a half-pint (150 ml) sized beaker to bale water 80 times in a minute from the full bowl to the empty one. Ask a friend to time you. How tired is your arm?

Every minute, your heart pumps this much blood.

Blood science

The heart has a muscle that never gets tired. It can pump away for a whole lifetime without ever needing a vacation. It also pumps very hard – over 14,000 quarts a day. When the body is active it needs more oxygen, which is absorbed through the lungs and carried in the blood. Then the heart must beat even faster to get blood around the body.

Pump power

As a rule of thumb, bigger animals have slower heartbeats than smaller ones. For example, adult humans have slower rates than children and babies. This huge elephant has a heart that dawdles along at about 25 to 30 beats per minute.

The tiny mouse's heart races at about 500 beats per minute.

Did you know?

If the inner surfaces of your lungs were laid out flat, they would cover an area more than two-thirds the size of a tennis court!

Seeing Sound

SOUNDS ACTUALLY MAKE THINGS MOVE, and although you can't really see sound, you sure can see how it works. These experiments show that there really are sound waves bouncing through the air.

Sound-wave science

The cookie sheet keeps on vibrating after you have hit it with the spoon. As it vibrates, so does the air around it, and these small vibrations, called sound waves, spread out in all directions. When the sound waves reach the drum they start it vibrating too and make the sugar jump up and down. Some of the sound waves also hit the drum in your ear (your "eardrum") and when that vibrates your brain interprets it as sound.

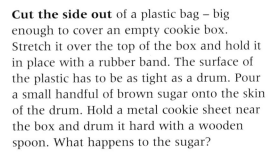

Sound waves travel through air and make the cookie box skin vibrate.

As you whack the cookie sheet, it vibrates and creates sound waves

Cut the side out of a plastic bag – big enough to cover an empty cookie box. Stretch it over the top of the box and hold it in place with a rubber band. The surface of the plastic has to be as tight as a drum. Pour a small handful of brown sugar onto the skin of the drum. Hold a metal cookie sheet near the box and drum it hard with a wooden spoon. What happens to the sugar?

The sugar on top of the skin starts to jiggle up and down – dancing in time to the music.

Bang on the drum
All sounds are made because something vibrates – sometimes you see the vibrations and sometimes you don't. When these kettle drums are bashed you can see the skins move, sending out some huge sound waves.

Air gun

Here's how to make an air gun that can blow out a candle. But the bullets it fires are blasts of sound.

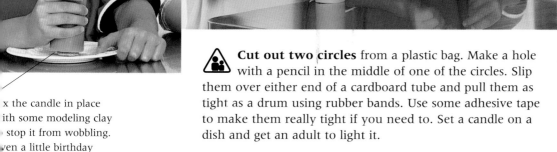

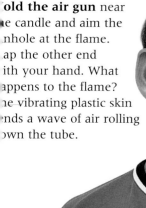

...x the candle in place ...ith some modeling clay ...o stop it from wobbling. ...ven a little birthday ...ke candle would do.

...old the air gun near ...e candle and aim the ...nhole at the flame. ...ap the other end ...ith your hand. What ...appens to the flame? ...e vibrating plastic skin ...nds a wave of air rolling ...own the tube.

Cut out two circles from a plastic bag. Make a hole with a pencil in the middle of one of the circles. Slip them over either end of a cardboard tube and pull them as tight as a drum using rubber bands. Use some adhesive tape to make them really tight if you need to. Set a candle on a dish and get an adult to light it.

Sounds powerful

If sound waves can blow out a candle and make sugar dance up and down, what else can they do? Loud sounds can make a teetering bank of snow start to slide down a mountain. It's what makes some avalanches come crashing down. Oil explorers explode dynamite to bounce sound waves off layers of underground rock. By studying the echoes they can tell where pools of oil may lie.

Fast sounds

The roar of a plane's jet engines is so loud it would deafen airport workers unless they wore hearing protectors. Sound travels through air at about 1,115 ft (340 m) a second (a little bit faster than most passenger jets). In seawater it goes five times faster still. Warships send sound waves (sonar) into the sea to find underwater enemies – like submarines.

When the wave hits the small hole it shoots out hard enough to blow out the candle.

After Dark

IF SOMEONE TOLD YOU THAT people can hardly see a thing by daylight, you would think they were crazy. But it's true. By day we can only see one star in the universe, the Sun, but by night we can see zillions. So if you really want to find out more about the universe, stay up late.

Moon science

As the Moon circles the Earth it changes shape day by day. Not a clever trick, just the way the Moon sails in and out of the shadow of the Earth while it orbits us. The changing shapes are called the "phases" of the Moon.

Full Moon

Waning Gibbous

Waxing Gibbous

Last Quarter

First Quarter

Waning Crescent

New Moon
(not visible from Earth)

Waxing Crescent

Ocean of Storms

Moon watch

The best way to study the Moon is flat on your back looking through a pair of binoculars on a clear night. Track the changing shapes of the Moon (phases) and fill in this Moon chart of a lunar month.

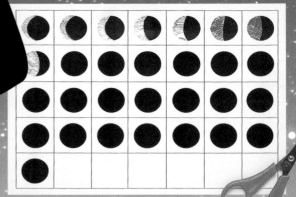

Draw up a chart with seven columns and five rows. Draw 29 black circles in each box. Every night, cut the Moon's shape out of aluminum foil and stick it onto a black circle. How long until the Moon looks like it did in the first box again? (This is because it has completed one orbit of the Earth.)

Sea of Rains

Appenine Mountains

Sea of Serenity

Copernicus
Crater

Sea of Vapors

Sea of Tranquility

Ptolomaeus
Crater

Sea of Clouds

Tycho
Crater

Moonscapes

The Moon is the nearest thing in the sky. On a clear night you can see surprising details. The best time to study the Moon is when it's growing from a crescent shape to a full circle – that's when it is visible at the right time of night. The seas are plains of dark lava (people once thought they held water). At full Moon watch for the bright rays that extend from the crater Tycho.

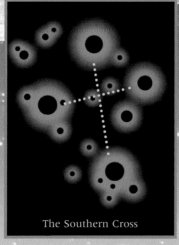

Polaris
(The North
Star)

The Plow

The Southern Cross

Compass stars

If you are in the Northern Hemisphere, face north using a compass, then look up slowly, and you will see the North Star. If you are in the Southern Hemisphere, aim the compass south to find the Southern Cross.

Did you know?

Did you know that on Earth we only ever see one side of the Moon? The only humans who have ever seen the other side are astronauts who have flown around it.

Sky racers

When meteors enter Earth's atmosphere they heat up and burn. This makes them appear to streak across the sky at night. We call these "shooting stars." Look out for them low on the horizon.

Night sight

It takes about half an hour for eyes to adjust to the dark in order to see faint stars. So if you want to make notes or study a star map, you'll need a night light. Cover the lens of a flashlight with red cellophane and tape it down tightly. The red glow is so dim that it won't wipe out your night vision.

Hearing Things

YOU ONLY HEAR SOUNDS because vibrating air hits your ears. Sound is made when something vibrates – the air around it mov back and forth and creates sound waves.

Earphones

Sound waves can travel through solids as well as air. So a piece of string is fine if you want to make a simple phone. This one is great for secrets since it lets you whisper to a friend without anybody overhearing.

Poke a small hole carefully in the bottom of two plastic cups (yogurt cups would be fine) with a sharp pencil or a pen.

Take a 15 ft (5 m) length of string. Wet an end and twirl it into a point. Thread it through the hole in one cup.

Tie a paper clip to the end of the string so that it doesn't slip out of the hole. Do the same with the other cup.

Don't let the string sag or the vibrations will peter out part way across.

Tell your friend to take one phone and walk backward until the string is tight. Now make a long distance call. As you speak your voice makes the air in the cup vibrate. The string starts to vibrate too. The vibrations travel down the string. At the other end the cup vibrates and so does the air inside it. Now your friend can hear what you are saying.

The smallest bones

in your body

are in your ears

Rack and roll

Here's proof that sound travels better through solid things than through air.

Try playing with other objects to see if the sound changes. Different utensils will make higher or lower sounds.

Pull a couple of coat hangers into diamond shapes. Hook the hooks onto a metal oven rack. Hang the other ends from your fingers. Put your fingers in your ears. Now get a friend to "play" the oven rack with a wooden spoon. Loud, isn't it? That's because the sound waves go straight from solid metal to the solid bone of your head – and into your inner ears.

High-sounding science

The closer together sound waves flow, the higher the sound they make. This is known as high pitched sound. In the row of bottles below, the less air there is, the higher the pitch. That's why the bottle with the most water gives the highest note.

Add a bit of food coloring for more colorful sounds.

High five

Get together a few bottles of the same size, put different amounts of water in them, and test their pitch. Blow across the top of the bottles to start the air inside vibrating. Listen to the different sounds. Which bottle makes the highest sound?

Hearing science

When someone speaks to you, vibrating waves of air hit your ears and set your eardrum jiggling back and forth. It pushes on the tiniest bones of your body – those of the middle ear – and on the inner ear, too. There, cells tipped with tiny hairs turn the waves into nerve signals that zip off to the brain.

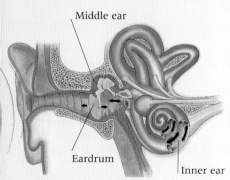

Middle ear

Eardrum

Inner ear

91

Index

Acknowledgments

Chris Maynard has written more than 55 children's books. He won the Rhone-Poulenc Science Junior Book of the Year in 1996 for *The World of Weather* and his *Informania Sharks* was runner up for the TES Senior Information Book Award in 1998. Recently, he has discovered the joys of writing Web sites too.

The publisher would like to thank the following people for their help in the production of this book: Janet Allis for additional design help, Andy Crawford for additional photography, Tracey Simmonds for photography assistance, Trish Gant and Gary Ombl for additional photography, Lara Tankel Holtz for the loan of her yard and kitchen, Adrian Hall Garden Centres for the equipment, Suzie Leaman for her help and understanding during the photo sessions, and the parents of all the budding scientists.

Picture Credits

The publisher would like to thank the following for their kind permission to reproduce their images:

Position key: c=center; b=bottom; l=left; r=right; t=top.

Bitstock-ifa: Number Three Co 16c; 62cl. **Corbis UK Ltd**: Roger Garwood & Trish Ainslie 53cr. **Image Bank**: 62bl, 62cl (above), 75cr. **Robert Harding Picture Library**: Nedra Westwater 56bl. **N.A.S.A.**: 53br. **N.H.P.A.**: 21cr; E A James 17cr; Stephen Dalton 37br, 40tr. **Powerstock Photolibrary / Zefa**: 3r. **Science Photo Library**: Microfield Scientific Ltd 26br; Peter Ryan 79cr; Professor P. Motta 82cr; 13tr; Andrew Syred 65cr; Claude Nuridsany and Maria Pennous 69c(above); Dr Fred Espenak 57cr(above); John Sanford 88-89, 89t; Keith Kent 41crb. **Silly Putty:** Silly Putty is registered trademark of Binney Smith, used with permission 15cr.

gettyone stone: 6tr, 29cr; Darrell Gulin Endpapers; J F Causse 16tr; J. F. Causse 56tr; Michael Orton 2c; Oliver Strewe 48c. **Telegraph Colour Library**: John Wilkes 49tr; Tony Bennett 41cb; Ivar Mjell 71cr; P.Gridley 87cr. **Woodfall Wild Images**: 9br.